The Illustrated Guide to

ASTROLOGY

JUDY HALL

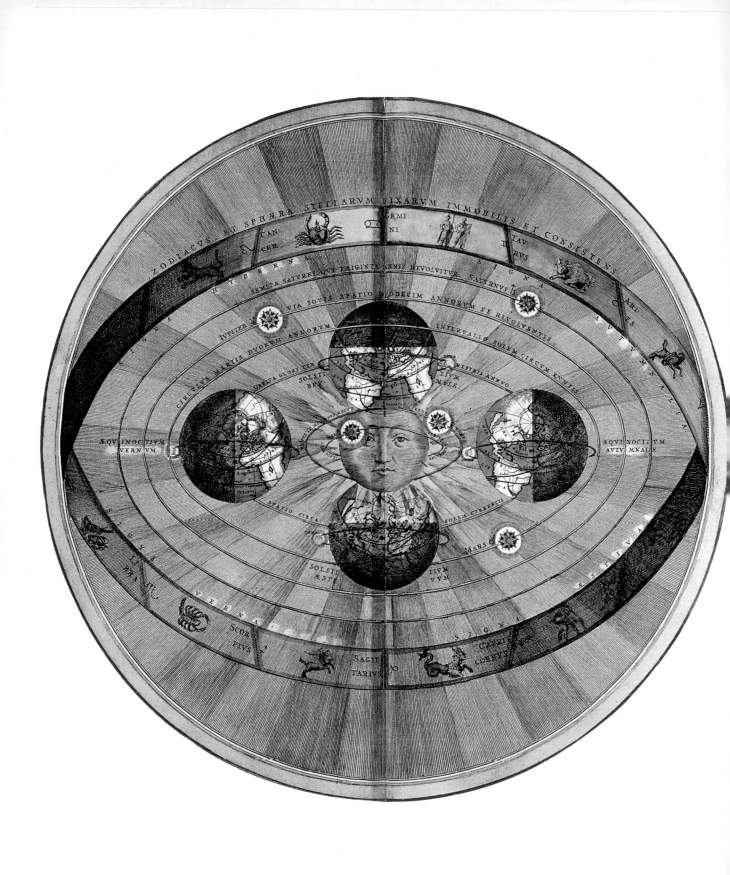

The Illustrated Guide to

ASTROLOGY

JUDY HALL

 A GODSFIELD BOOK

First published in Great Britain in 1999
by Godsfield Press Ltd
A division of David and Charles Ltd
Laurel House, Station Approach,
New Alresford, Hants SO24 9JY, UK

10 9 8 7 6 5 4 3 2 1

Designed for Godsfield Press by
The Bridgewater Book Company

Picture research by Liz Eddison

Printed and bound in Hong Kong

ISBN 1–899434–53-4

PRECEDING PAGE: *A seventeenth-century map of
the heavens showing the constellations of
the zodiac around the edge.*

Contents

Traditional Astrology

Astrology is an ancient art, but one that has relevance to your life today. It can identify areas of compatibility and conflict, indicate the perfect timing for an enterprise, point you in the right direction if you wish to move house or change career, and even suggest what you did in a previous life. Above all, astrology helps you to know yourself – and others.

ANCIENT TIMES

Astrology has been used over aeons of time. Thirty-five thousand years ago, early man – or was it woman? – scratched a Moon calendar onto a piece of bone to show the phases of the Moon. The Moon was a magical, mystical object. Worshiped for its life-giving powers, the waxing and waning of the Moon symbolized birth, death, and rebirth. It kept track of fertility, showed when to plant and harvest, and guided the hunter. Small wonder, then, that when Stonehenge was built over 20.000 years later, it was a lunar and solar observatory set out in stone. Similar observations are recorded all over the ancient world.

In ancient times, no division was made between astrology and astronomy. In Babylon, Arabia, China, and Egypt sky maps enabled the astronomer-priests to calculate propitious timings for affairs of state. The astronomy was surprisingly sophisticated: not only did the ancients keep track of eclipses, but they mapped events that occurred over millennia, and, as the sky maps on Egyptian temples and tombs show, were clearly aware of events in deepest space, far out of reach of all but the most modern telescope.

Stonehenge is an ancient solar and lunar landscape, the sky is reflected on the ground. It accurately predicts eclipses and other astronomical events.

THE MEDIEVAL EXPERIENCE

In medieval Europe, and a little later in America, astrology pervaded all aspects of life. Astrology was not always condemned by the Church. Pope Sixtus IV was the first of several popes to draw up and interpret a birthchart.

Astrology not only predicted events, but diagnosed and treated medical conditions. Herbs were grown, harvested, and prescribed according to strict astrological rules. Patients, from peasants to royalty, had a chart drawn up the moment an illness struck and they were given an herbal mixture based on that chart – in much the same way that a body scan is used to identify and diagnose necessary treatment today.

Medieval astrologers made some pretty accurate predictions, too. Nostradamus is perhaps the best-known astrologer, although he had to disguise his predictions in obscure "quartets" to avoid the attention of the Inquisition. One French king had reason to rue the day he ignored the astrologer's warning. Told that, at a specific time, day, and place, he would be "cruelly killed" when something pierced the "golden cage" around his head, the King nevertheless went off to joust. His gilded helmet could well be described as a "golden cage." The "something sharp" was his opponent's lance, which pierced his eye socket. The king duly died, in agony.

The royal courts of Europe each had their own astrologer, and Popes, too, practiced this arcane art.

The American constitution's astrological basis is reflected by the stars on its flag.

ASTROLOGY AND THE NEW WORLD

Astrology was taken to the New World by the early settlers, many of whom were seeking freedom for their beliefs. The signing of the American Declaration of Independence and the setting up of the new Constitution were carefully calculated for the most propitious astrological moment.

Modern Astrology

♈ Aries

♉ Taurus

♊ Gemini

♋ Cancer

♌ Leo

♍ Virgo

♎ Libra

♏ Scorpio

♐ Sagittarius

♑ Capricorn

♒ Aquarius

♓ Pisces

The symbols for the signs of the zodiac are called glyphs or sigils.

In recent times astrology has enjoyed a resurgence of interest. It is now used as a psychological and counseling tool, to make business decisions, and to guide careers. Astrologers have advised a president and a princess. More and more people are turning to this practical tool for enhancing their lives.

YOUR SUN-SIGN

Most people today are familiar with their "stars," the Sun-sign forecasts found in newspapers and magazines. The forecasts are based on the zodiac sign in which the Sun was placed at your birth. Sun-sign astrology is generalized, so that while it may be uncannily accurate for a few people, it cannot predict successfully for everyone. You need a birthchart calculated for the moment of birth if you are to fully understand what the planets have in store.

Knowing your Sun-sign can, however, tell you a great deal about yourself. People born under the same sign share certain characteristics and approach life in the same way. They have similar aspirations and ambitions, and their personalities are broadly similar. So, if you know a person's Sun-sign, you know a great deal about them.

USING ASTROLOGY

Astrology, however, is much more than just the Sun-sign. When you know where the planets were at your birth, you have a map of your own inner dynamics. Crack the code, and you have the key to understanding yourself. Compare your chart with that of another person, and you know where your personalities blend and where they will clash. Observe the movement of the planets overhead, and you understand where your future is going.

Astrology can answer many questions and there are specialist fields of astrology, dealing with different aspects. If you know the kind of astrologer you need, you can illuminate different areas of your life. And if you understand the fundamentals of astrology, you can work out the answers to some of those questions for yourself.

The siege of Troy started because the goddess of love, Venus, was a jealous loser. Faced with a woman more beautiful than herself, she incited a nation to war.

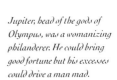

Jupiter, head of the gods of Olympus, was a womanizing philanderer. He could bring good fortune but his excesses could drive a man mad.

MYTHOLOGY

Modern astrology has its roots in Greece and Rome. The Astrologers of that time attributed to each planet an individual and unique personality that was mirrored in the gods and goddesses of the day. These gods were not remote figures – they interacted with, and interfered in, the affairs of men. As the myths show, they were far from perfect, but on the contrary were capricious, contrary, and all too human. The gods had love affairs, were betrayed, and took their revenge. They fought just as often as they loved, and they bestowed their kindness, or animosity, merely on a whim.

The goddess of love

Venus (or Aphrodite) could be romantic and pleasure-loving, but she could also be erotic, jealous and even murderous. The myths tell us that the Trojan War started because of a beauty contest: Venus was so furious at not being chosen the most beautiful woman that she vowed vengeance on the winner, Helen.

Understanding Astrology

Astrology is based on the principle: "As above, so below. As within, so without." The map of the heavens overhead at the moment of your birth is a map of your psyche. Your inner dynamics are reflected in the position of the planets above you. This means that astrology is not something set apart from you, it is you. Where the Sun and the other planets were at your moment of birth give you a unique personality. How those planets move and interweave affects the course of your life.

THE SCIENCE OF ASTROLOGY

The science of astrology lies in beautifully precise maps of planetary movements. The journey of the stars around the heavens, as seen from the perspective of earth, is called the zodiac. The map of your own particular journey is called your birthchart. The science of astrology will tell you when and how the patterns in your birthchart unfold throughout your life.

The science of astrology states that, on a certain day each year, the Sun will be in a particular sign of the zodiac. It also states that, because planetary movements do not exactly coincide with calendar time, the day on which the Sun moves into a certain sign varies slightly over a four-year period. The science is also aware that the astrological Sun and the astronomical Sun differ. Due to a technicality called The Precession of the Equinoxes, the Sun also moves around the zodiac in a greater, 25,000 year, cycle. Instead of recalculating the tables of planetary movements, astrology uses a symbolic zodiac.

THE ART OF ASTROLOGY

The art of astrology lies in interpreting and synthesizing the components of your own unique chart, and in blending it with that of another person. This book will help you to do this.

A horoscope is calculated for the moment of birth but sets out the course of a life.

In astrological terms, the Sun, Moon, and the planets revolve around the earth. A horoscope places the planets as they appear viewed from the earth. Each moment is different as the planets all move at differing speeds, constantly creating a new pattern.

	Sun-sign dates	**Signs**	**Ruling Planet**
Aries	March 21 – April 19	Aries ♈	Sun ☉
Taurus	April 20 – May 20	Taurus ♉	Moon ☽
Gemini	May 21 – June 20	Gemini ♊	Mercury ☿
Cancer	June 21 – July 22	Cancer ♋	Venus ♀
Leo	July 23 – Aug 22	Leo ♌	Mars ♂
Virgo	Aug 23 – Sept 22	Virgo ♍	Jupiter ♃
Libra	Sept 23 – Oct 22	Libra ♎	Saturn ♄
Scorpio	Oct 23 – Nov 21	Scorpio ♏	Chiron ⚷
Sagittarius	Nov 22 – Dec 21	Sagittarius ♐	Uranus ♅
Capricorn	Dec 22 – Jan 19	Capricorn ♑	Neptune ♆
Aquarius	Jan 20 – Feb 18	Aquarius ♒	Pluto ♇
Pisces	Feb 19 – March 20	Pisces ♓	North Node ☊

How to Use This Book

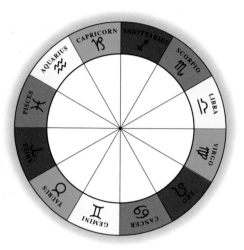

The Zodiac Wheel shows the path of the Sun over a year. The astrological year begins in March when the Sun moves into the astrological sign of Aries. The year closes with the Sun in the sign of Pisces (signs are read counterclockwise).

UNDERSTANDING YOURSELF

This book is divided into sections. The first section is based on your Sun-sign. If you are unsure of your Sun-sign, the table on page 11 tells you which sign of the zodiac the Sun was located in when you were born. Under your sign you will find details of your personality, your likes and dislikes, your needs and desires. (You will find out more about your approach to love in the compatibility section (see page 116). This section will also help you to spot the different Sun-signs, so that you can use it to understand other people.

The following sections introduce different facets of astrology, such as the Elements (see page 48) and the Qualities (see page 50), which help you to understand more about the way you function. In the planetary section (see page 54), tables indicate the sign in which your Moon was placed when you were born. (Most planets need a properly calculated birthchart to pinpoint position.) Understanding the position of planets refines the energies of your chart, taking you deeper into your inner dynamics. By calculating your Ascendant (see page 94), you can see how you approach the world. In understanding houses (see page 104), you know in which area of your life the planetary forces operate. The section "Putting it all Together" integrates the separate parts of your birthchart into a whole picture.

UNDERSTANDING OTHER PEOPLE

Looking up someone's Sun-sign helps you to get to know them better. By studying the compatibility section (see page 116) you will learn more about your own sexual and relationship needs, and identify where you harmonize and where you clash with other signs. Certain signs approach life from a totally opposite direction to others. If you are aware of this, you can make allowances for individual differences, and as a result bring much greater acceptance into your relationships.

WHAT IS A BIRTHCHART?

A birthchart reflects the moment of your birth. To calculate a birthchart you need to know three things: your time of birth, the place, and the date. Your birthchart shows the layout of the planets in the skies overhead at that

Astrological charts reflect the similarities, and the differences, between two people.

Computers quickly calculate and print a chart, showing signs, planets, angles, and aspects.

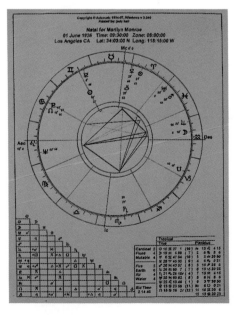

moment. It is what you would have observed when you opened your eyes and saw the heavens above, and what would have been hidden from sight below the horizon. Wherever you are born, the planets appear to be moving around you. This is why astrology looks at the planets as moving around the Earth, not the Sun. So, the Sun is marked on your chart as traveling around the center point. That center point is either the Earth or you, whichever you find it easier to imagine.

Computer charts

You do not need a birthchart to use this book, but if you do have one it will help you to understand yourself even better. Computer-generated charts are easily obtainable from the addresses given on page 128.

What Can Astrology Do?

Astrology is a highly versatile tool: apart from helping you to understand yourself and other people better, it can answer a clear-cut question, advise you on your love life, point you toward a suitable career, find you a new place to live, resolve areas of conflict, and much more!

PERSONALITY TYPES

Astrology is one of the best ways to understand what makes people tick. No one reveals the whole of themselves at a first meeting, but once you understand astrology and how to combine the different factors, you can look behind the façade of a person to recognize who they really are.

As we shall see, the zodiac has 12 fundamental personality types based on Sun-sign characteristics. This basic personality type is mediated by several factors, one of the most important of which is the Moon. Once you have begun to understand how the Moon colors the basic Sun-sign, then you understand not just 12 personas but 144 different personality types. Add to that the 12 possible outlooks that the Ascendant represents for each of those personalities and you begin to see just how subtle and complex an understanding astrology can offer.

NATAL ASTROLOGY

Natal astrology is the art of looking at your birthchart and seeing your self and your life unfolding in front you. It helps you to understand yourself better, to recognize your strengths and weaknesses and to take advantage of opportunities for growth as they arise. It can also offer specific advice on areas such as relationships or your career.

Astrology pinpoints specific characteristics and traits shared by everyone born under a particular sign.

How you move forward in life is shown by your astrological chart, which can guide your choice of career.

CAREER GUIDANCE

Astrologers have always associated particular Sun-signs with certain types of career. In medieval times, Aries was the knight on a white charger rushing off to right the wrongs of the world. A little later, Aries was riding the wagon train out to conquer the Wild West, or panning for gold in a mountain stream. Nowadays the white charger might have become a flashy sports car, but Aries still has that fighting spirit. An astrologer would suggest a career as a racing driver, entrepreneur, metalworker, soldier, butcher, electrician, or surveyor. (You will find suitable professions for your Sun-sign listed later in the book.)

PREDICTIVE ASTROLOGY

The reason why people read their Sun-sign horoscopes in the newspapers is that they are curious to know what is going to happen to them. Everyone would like a little light shed on their future, and many people consult an astrologer for this very purpose. Astrologers observe the day-to-day movement of the planets and calculate how that movement will affect either the Sun-sign or the natal chart. They can foresee changes, opportunities, blocks, and events such as marriage or birth. Astrologers realize that today we have more control over our own lives than ever before, so astrology is moving from a sense of preordained fate toward the astrology of choice and freewill. Astrologers now look at tendencies and possibilities instead of predicting events that are written in stone.

HORARY ASTROLOGY

If you have a precise and specific question, then horary astrology is for you. The astrologer takes the exact time when the question was asked and applies a set of "rules" to arrive at an answer. This type of astrology is particularly useful when you have questions such as: "Should I buy this house?", "Will I pass my examination?", or "Will I marry the person I have just met?"

KARMIC ASTROLOGY

Karmic astrology seeks answers to present-life problems in past lives. It looks at the credits and deficits that have been carried from life to life, examines in-built patterns of emotional expectation, and suggests what some of those past lives may have been like. It can be used to help you understand relationships, vocations, family life and patterns of disease better.

ELECTIONAL ASTROLOGY

If timing is important to you, then electional astrology is what you need. This branch of astrology looks at propitious moments. So, if you want to know a good day on which to get married or start up a new business, consult an electional astrologer. A chart will be prepared for several possible dates and then the best one can be selected. The final choice is up to you.

ASTROCARTOGRAPHY (OR LOCATION ASTROLOGY)

If you cannot decide where to live, or want to know where to make things happen, then astrocartography may help you. A map of your chart is superimposed over a map of the world, and the result is a cascade of lines passing through different countries. The astrocartographer will tell you which planetary line is best for different purposes. If you want to meet a new partner, for example, then you may like go on a vacation where your Venus line crosses your Jupiter line. But

Horary astrology tells you whether it would be wise to buy a house, electional astrology the best time to make the move.

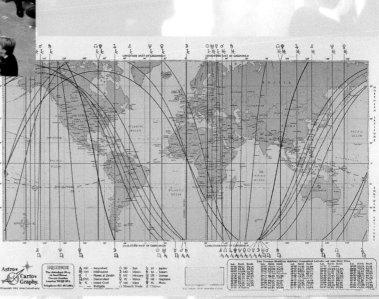

Astrology is increasingly used to help business plan strategies – and to find the right employee.

if you want the relationship to last, you may have to follow your Saturn line. Astrocartography is a complex process, but you can obtain charts by mail order (see page 128) with explanations of what the different lines mean. It is also possible to ask specifically: "Where in the world would it be best for me to live if I want to . . ."

MUNDANE ASTROLOGY

Mundane astrology incorporates separate, specialized fields of astrology, such as finance and politics. It is concerned with world events, and social and financial trends. Specialist astrologers can predict the movement of stocks and shares with reliable accuracy and many businesses take advantage of this advice. Others look at wider social needs and examine ways of meeting these.

Astrologers have also been working on forecasting weather and earth activity, such as earthquakes. With computers speeding up research and enabling vast quantities of data to be handled at any one time, these areas will no doubt expand as astrology moves into a new millennium.

If you want to know where to meet a prospective partner, astrocartography will pinpoint exactly the right place – but you might need to travel quite a distance!

BUSINESS ASTROLOGY

Business astrology is a rapidly growing field of expertise. Applications range from personality profiles on prospective employees, to financial and marketing trends and advice on when to buy or sell assets. Many businesses actually employ their own astrologer – the same way ancient kings did!

FINDING AN ASTROLOGER

Choosing the right astrologer is the key to a successful enquiry. Professional training is available in all branches of astrology. Training schools advertise in astrological magazines. Astrological Associations have lists of members – all of whom will be reputable and well qualified.

Your Questions Answered

There are certain questions that inevitably arise whenever astrology is discussed, and perennial misunderstandings that occur when rational "science" looks at its ancient ancestor. All have a reasonable explanation.

"Astronomers say that the zodiac signs are all wrong. What is going on?"
From Earth, the point where the astronomical sun rises at the spring equinox appears to move slowly backward through the zodiac. Therefore the present position of the signs is different from where they were in ancient times. Astrologers are well aware that their zodiac no longer conforms to the sky overhead. A symbolic zodiac is used where the Sun always rises at 0° Aries at the spring equinox.

"Aren't there are more than 12 constellations along the Sun's path?"
Astrologers know that there are other constellations that intrude into the path of the Sun. But the Sun passes quickly through these areas and so the only signs used are those that allow the Sun to make a uniform progress.

Astronomers spend considerable time studying the heavens and new discoveries are always just on the horizon. Astrologers use a zodiac which was laid down thousands of years ago.

The constantly changing sky is carefully divided into 12 equal areas to form the astrological zodiac.

"Why do astrologers draw a chart as though the Sun moves around the Earth. Surely they know it is the other way around?"

Yes, they do. Charts are drawn from the perspective of our vantage point on Earth. The planets *appear* to move around the Earth – some are visible, others are not. A birthchart shows those that are visible in the top half of the chart, and those that are not in the bottom.

"I read my horoscope but it never seems to work for me."

Sun-sign columns are calculated in the most general terms. If you were born in the middle of a sign, then they may well work. But if you were born a quarter or three-quarters of the way through, then the timing can be wrong. These forecasts also take into account the movement of a planet into or out of a sign. So, if you are born right at the beginning or end it may work. But elsewhere, you will have to wait weeks, months, even years before the effect is felt.

"I read my Sun-sign but it doesn't sound like me!"

If you were born very close to the beginning or end of a sign, you might actually find that you belong to the sign preceding, or the one following. Another explanation is that a particular planet may be strong in your chart and it overshadows your Sun-sign. A personalized natal chart will give you the answers. Signs, as well as people, have their "shadow side." If qualities that did not fit in with your parents' idea of what a child should be were particularly strong in you, you could well have been educated out of being your natural self. Knowing all about your Sun-sign gives you the opportunity to shine.

"I sent for a horoscope interpretation by post and it has conflicts, especially when it comes to the future!"

The interpretation was done by a computer! An astrologer weighs up different factors and judges which will be stronger or most likely. A computer cannot do this – on one day you might find yourself facing a glorious opportunity for travel and fun, and the need to retreat from the world.

Sun-sign forecasts can be amusing – and may occasionally be accurate – but they shouldn't be taken too seriously!

The 12 zodiac constellations are pictured as mythical beasts or emblems.

Aries   *Taurus*

Gemini   *Cancer*

Leo   *Virgo*

Libra   *Scorpio*

Sagittarius   *Capricorn*

Aquarius   *Pisces*

The Zodiac Signs

When ancient man looked at the stars he identified the constellations stretching along the path of the Sun as the celestial zodiac, picturing them as mythical beasts and emblems. This imaginary and symbolic band was split into 12 equal divisions, known as the signs of the zodiac. Astrologically speaking, each of these signs represents a segment of the whole gamut of human experience. The individual signs have a precise meaning and specific correspondences.

A CELESTIAL JOURNEY

The zodiac is not only the celestial path of the Sun, it is a voyage through human experience. In metaphysical teaching, it represents the journey of the soul (the Sun) through incarnation from childhood to old age.

In Aries, the first sign of the zodiac, a soul comes into incarnation. This is the sign of initiation and new beginnings. This is where "I" begins – the consciousness of self. In Taurus the soul learns about being in a physical body and using its resources and senses to interact with the world. This is where the life force becomes material substance. By the time we reach Gemini, the soul is learning to communicate, the urge is toward self-expression. In maternal Cancer the instinct is to nurture; in Leo it is to shine forth and be recognized – this sign is the natural ruler of the zodiac. Virgo, on the other hand, is the urge to be of service to one's fellow humans.

By the time Libra is reached, halfway around the zodiac, the process of self-consciousness is complete. Young adulthood has been reached. Now it is time to enter into a relationship, to explore unity: Libra is the place where the soul meets itself in another. Scorpio is the place of sex, death, and rebirth: this sign has to master creative power. In Sagittarius the urge is toward meaning: this philosophical sign is on an eternal quest for understanding. When we reach Capricorn, the urge is for an ordered, stable society: the "We" of Libra becomes "Us," the wider group. This is the drive toward authority and control. In humanitarian Aquarius, the concern is for the good of the whole. Visionary Pisces longs to return, to merge back into the Oneness from which it all started – or to escape from the eternal round.

♍ ♎ ♏ ♐ ♑ ♒ ♓

The Sun is the indicator of a unique approach to the world – focused through a sign of the zodiac.

SUN-SIGN ASTROLOGY

As the Sun enters the different signs, it takes on the energy and coloring of the sign. Each sign of the zodiac represents a unique personality, a particular way of viewing the world, a specific challenge and certain needs, drives, and desires. The Sun in a sign imparts a distinctive appearance and predisposes one toward certain behavior patterns. So, your Sun-sign can tell you a lot about yourself and can help you to understand not only yourself, but the people around you.

Even small children display the characteristics of their Sun-sign. Some have a sunny nature, others are obstinate or demanding.

♈ | Aries

THE RAM

Bold, brash, and pushy are the Aries qualities most people remember. There is little subtlety about Aries – what you see is what you get. This sign is confident, courageous, and strongly motivated. This is the "Me" sign of the zodiac. "I think you'll find I'm right" is the cry. As an impulsive and competitive Aries you are enterprising but self-orientated. You have an urge to make your mark upon the world, to get things moving – fast!

THE SYMBOL

The Ram is your symbol. Like a ram, you will not hesitate to lock horns with an adversary. You need to be leader of the pack.

PERSONALITY

Aries' personality is strong, pushy, and difficult to ignore. Frank and open, you say what you think with confidence. Headstrong and dynamic, you move through life like a whirlwind, sweeping all before you. Action rather than introspection is your strongest urge.

You are naturally assertive and competitive, enjoying meeting life's challenges. Always active, you seek out adventure and excitement. Nothing boring or mundane will suit your fiery nature. A natural initiator, you have a tendency to rush into things, but may well lack the tenacity to see them through.

You truly believe you are right and that you know best. Combine this with the independent nature of Aries, and you have a personality that prefers to do things alone. Aries is rarely a team player – unless you can be out front leading!

As an Aries, you need to be the dominant leader of the pack, just like your symbol – the Ram.

Fiery and assertive, Aries makes an impact. It is hard to overlook this bold fire sign.

APPEARANCE

Aries radiates energy and has a lean, athletic body that looks set to take off at any moment. There is a certain cockiness about the confident Aries stance. One of the most striking features about an Aries face is the bold "ram's horn" eyebrows that dominate a strong forehead.

CAREER

Aries relishes a challenge – the bold cut and thrust of competition turns you on. Unfortunately there are not enough jobs as racing car drivers, test pilots, and astronauts to satisfy your demand for excitement, so you have to fall back on fire-fighting, aggressive driving, selling, fighting, wheeling and dealing. Your flair for spotting an opening makes you an excellent entrepreneur and your ability to fight means you rarely lose out to a competitor. With your independent nature, you want to be in business for yourself. If you do work for a company, it needs to be dynamic and at the cutting edge. You may well enjoy the excitement of the money market, buying and selling commodities of all kinds. More mundane aspects, like book-keeping, are not for you. With your predilection for taking risks, the job of insurance assessor or surveyor may be right up your street. With your love for striking a good deal, the world is your oyster.

Aries has an affinity with all things sharp and cutting. Traditional occupations include surgeon and butcher. You also have a connection with electricity and with metal, so a career in these fields will engage your interest – vital if you are to stick with the job.

Sparks fly when an Aries is around. Hazardous occupations are your forte.

♉ | Taurus

THE BULL

As a Taurus, you are strong and tenacious – nothing pushes you off track – just like your symbol: the bull.

Loyal, dependable, steadfast, and enduring are key words for Taurus. Rooted in security and stability, the material world is your natural environment. "Mine" is a favorite word. You find your security, and your motivation, in your partner, your house, and your work. Outer practicality often conceals an artistic and hedonistic nature. You approach life cautiously but with great tenacity. Nothing pushes a Taurus off track when you make your mind up!

THE SYMBOL

The bull is your symbol. Like the bull, you are strong, determined, and stubborn. Other signs should beware when you start to paw the ground – a Taurean is slow to rouse but unstoppable when in motion.

PERSONALITY

The Taurean personality is characterized by fixity of intent and steadfastness of purpose. You enjoy an orderly routine and a sense of security – uncertainty and risk-taking do not suit you. Valuing integrity, you can be relied upon; given a task, you carry it through to the very end. You are loyal and faithful, and you dislike change.

This fixity is often your downfall. Finding it difficult to change your mind, you may dig a grave for yourself by your stubborn adherence to your duty and responsibilities, and your inflexible ideas. This dogged determination makes you appear intolerant and intransigent, but it is more that you find it difficult to put yourself in someone else's place and see things from their point of view – especially when this challenges your own view of life.

Taureans have a possessive and jealous nature. You like to hold onto what you perceive as yours, whether this be possessions or people. Nevertheless, you are surprisingly hedonistic and can be generous in sharing your pleasure with others. Your love of fine things means that you are not afraid to indulge yourself – indeed, you surround yourself with the best you can afford.

APPEARANCE

Taurus has a strong, earthy appearance. You stand firm but may appear indolent because you move slowly but with purpose – unless strongly aroused, when a raging bull is let loose. Your body is stocky, but tapers down to slender ankles and feet. You have a large, well-shaped head, melting eyes, and a long neck that dominates powerful shoulders. Your most striking feature is your mellifluous voice.

Taureans enjoy possessions and often use their artistic eye to collect or deal in antiques.

CAREER

As Taurus has an excellent singing voice, you find a creative and lucrative outlet through music and the associated arts. With your excellent eye for quality, you are successful as an art or antiques dealer, a merchandizer or a manufacturer. Practical and productive, you fit easily into a team situation.

Taurus has a strong affinity with money – you like to have it and to hold onto it. So a good career would be banking, pensions, insurance or investment broking – but not for you the risk of the money market. A job as a property dealer, real estate agent or office manager would also appeal to you.

Structure matters to you, so architecture and building work offer scope for your talents, as does sculpture. With your practical, earthy nature, horticulture, farming, and forestry bring you close to the soil.

Wood-carving, sculpture, and pottery provide outlets for a Taurean's sense of structure and order.

♊ | Gemini

Inquisitive and playful, Gemini appears to possess the secret of eternal youth. This sociable sign has an unstoppable urge to communicate, question, and explore. "Listen to me!" you cry. With a tongue of quicksilver and a lively wit, you are an entertaining companion, until you get bored – which happens very quickly. Then the other side of your nature emerges and your tongue becomes deadly: gossip and sarcasm, elaboration and intrigue are all part of your multifaceted personality.

THE SYMBOL

The twins are the first human zodiac symbol and it is linked to the mind – an area that Geminis find endlessly fascinating. The duality of the sign indicates that there are at least two sides to everything for Gemini.

PERSONALITY

The Gemini personality is lively and versatile, with dazzling verbal skills. With your changeable and restless nature you rarely stay still for long and usually have several projects on the go. One of your most noticeable characteristics is knowing everything and everyone. A natural communicator, you gather in information, gossip, people, and an eclectic collection of gadgetry, all of which delight your natural curiosity and feed your insatiable need to know.

Ideas are the food of life to you, but the speed at which you move leads to a certain superficiality and inconsistency. You rarely stop to enquire deeply.

Of course, what you know is always right – until you change your mind. Not that you admit to mind-changing: somehow, when the subject comes around again, you argue from a different point of view. You won't like to be reminded of this and, with your silver tongue, you quickly convince people that you didn't actually *believe* it, but were just putting forward a theory. You can be equally flexible with the truth – duplicity is a side to your nature that you hide and use to your own advantage.

With such a restless nature, you are prone to nervous exhaustion. Pushing yourself to the limit depletes even your seemingly boundless energy, and the result is a crash into depression. But with your natural resilience, it isn't long before you spring back again.

Changeable Gemini has two sides – just like your symbol, the twins.

Mercury imparts a lively mind to Gemini, making you ideally suited to multi-tasking and adapting to ever-changing stimuli.

APPEARANCE

Youthful, birdlike, intellectual, animated – restless Gemini is most easily recognized by the speed at which you dart around doing several things at once. Your head is usually cocked to one side, your hands constantly gesture, your twinkling eyes flash everywhere – but the most telling indicator that you are a Gemini is that you never stop talking.

CAREER

Multitasking is your forte. Your versatile mind and ability to know everything and everyone at once makes you an ideal networker, journalist, teacher, broadcaster, writer, linguist, lawyer, advertising agent, publicist, personal assistant, computer operator, messenger, demonstrator, salesman, civil engineer – the list is endless!

With your manual dexterity, you excel at light assembly or craftwork, but should steer clear of anything repetitious. Look for something with variety, and you will be happy – for a while. Geminis will change their career more often than any other signs!

Gemini enjoys sharing knowledge – communication is the life blood of this intellectual sign.

THE LION

♌ | Leo

Regal Leo is hard to miss. You have a dramatic presence that makes people notice you – that and your tendency to organize their lives for them. "Come to me!" you roar. Proud, magnanimous, and brimming with enthusiasm, you want to enjoy life to the full and to share that joy with others. If they don't follow, you may well bully, or sulk. Warm-hearted Leo wants so very much to be special.

THE SYMBOL

The symbol for Leo is the proud, majestic lion. Just as the lion surveys its kingdom, you, too, look around your world with your head held high. You have to rule. A playful pussycat one moment, a fierce lion the next – woe betide people who offend your dignity. A haughty stare is usually enough to bring them to heel, but you won't hesitate to use the full power of your awesome might.

Proud lion or playful pussycat, like your symbol you are lion-hearted and proud.

PERSONALITY

Leo's personality is larger than life. A natural actor or actress, you crave applause. You have a deep need to be singled out as "special," to be noticed. If you are not, you create a scene – anything rather than be ignored.

Exuberant, enthusiastic, fiery, and generous, you are gregarious and outgoing, but strangely fixed and deeply opinionated. This is your inherent contradiction. Leo is a fixed sign, stubborn and determined. You want to be spontaneous, and yet your pride and deeply held beliefs hold you back. You find it difficult to change, locking into an inner conflict that can cause you to suffer from back or heart trouble.

Strong-willed, you expect a lot out of life and have a deep desire to be in control. At your worst you are pompous, bombastic, and snobbish. At your best you are creative, courageous, and generous. Your warm heart wants to bring sunshine into people's lives, but your need to dominate may overrule. Your strong principles lead you to fight for justice, just as long as it does not conflict with your own interests.

Leos love to be admired. Your
natural place is on a stage,
playing to an audience. Mae
West, a Leo, epitomizes
Leo's ostentatious style.

Proud and yet surprisingly sensitive, you can be easily hurt. You have a
deep need to feel special, and if other people misunderstand or ignore you,
then you feel deeply wounded – not that you will show it, for Leos rarely
reveal their pain.

APPEARANCE

The Leo mane predominates: a mass of hair flicked back with a sweeping
gesture. Proud, haughty, and self-assured, you survey the world
from a great height, even when your own stature is short. You
appear to be looking down on lesser mortals. Ostentatious
Leo likes gold – and flashy belt buckles. Even the poorest Leo
will wear costume jewelry but prefers the real thing.

William Jefferson Clinton,
a typical Leo dominating
the world stage.

CAREER

Leo is made for the stage, be it the theater, television, the courtroom,
the boardroom, the professions or the politician's seat – anywhere
your natural acting ability and flair for oratory can be
heard, your desire to be in control can be exercised
and fulfilled.

Happiest in a leadership role, you can be a
team player as long as the leader has your respect.
You hate to feel bored and under-stimulated, so
your work must be congenial. It must also conform to what you regard as your station in life.
Manual labor and lowly tasks do not suit a Leo!

♍ | Virgo

THE VIRGIN

Modest, restrained, and discriminating, Virgo always strives for perfection. Your critical, exacting standards are applied to yourself and to those around you. You have a deep desire to serve, and your caring nature lends itself to helping those in need. Your excellent mind, organizational ability, and attention to detail make you both efficient and practical. Other signs often rely on meticulous Virgo to keep things running smoothly.

THE SYMBOL

In older times, the Corn Maiden was the symbol for Virgo. Fertile and fecund, she symbolized the harvest and fruitfulness in accordance with the earthy nature of your sign. Later the Virgin was adopted, bringing a sterile purity to an inherently sensual sign. The result is a deep conflict between your natural sexual instincts and an innate desire to remain pure and untouched – a conflict that can lead to prudishness.

PERSONALITY

Virgo is a perfectionist and works hard, which can result in workaholism and lead to mental stress. You set exacting standards for yourself and for others, and may be overly critical if those standards are not met. Lowering your expectations slightly would set more realistic, achievable goals.

You have a logical and discriminating mind, with a tendency to analyze and categorize. Valuing rationality and common sense, you pay a great deal of attention to detail. In striving for an orderly, organized life, however, you may become pernickety and pedantic.

Virgo is a fastidious sign and many Virgos have an obsessive interest in hygiene. This sign is known for its love of housekeeping and filing. If you are one of the Virgos who fails to live up to the these expectations, try not to be too hard on yourself.

In ancient times, corn symbolized the fertile fecundity of this earthy sign.

APPEARANCE

Virgo is a tidy sign. Dressing neatly with clean, beautifully cut hair add up to the good grooming you value. Your body is likely to be bony and angular. While some Virgos appear sharply intellectual, others have a sensual, earthy

Neat, efficient, and well-organized, Virgo is an excellent administrator.

quality. You burn nervous energy and may well have an edgy, stressed look. But one thing is certain, as a Virgo you are at home in your body — well-coordinated and efficient in your movements.

CAREER

With your meticulous attention to detail, research can be a rewarding career, as can analytical or computer science, data processing, market research, accountancy, editing, or proofreading. Teaching, particularly at the higher education level, will also appeal.

With Virgo's traditional links with health, a career in health or hygiene will utilize your need to serve others — pharmacy may fit the bill. You may also enjoy working for a charity or care organization because helping others is one of your strongest instincts.

A supporting role is often preferred to being "boss." Your organizational and people skills are good. Personnel and human resources will utilize your talents, as will management training. A number of secretaries and personal assistants are Virgos, and dedicated Virgos can be found wherever loyalty and discretion are required. You need a routine but, if you are to be truly happy, you also need variety and stimulation. Virgo does not like to be bored.

Health and hygiene is a Virgoan preoccupation that often leads to a career in medicine or science.

Libra

THE SCALES

Libra is the sign of marriage and partnership. You feel happiest when you are in a relationship. Fair-minded and equable, you need balance and harmony in your life. A natural diplomat, fair and impartial justice is important to you. Decisions are difficult: seeing all sides, you find it hard to come to a conclusion. Inevitably late for an appointment, you apologize with great charm and are quickly forgiven!

THE SYMBOL

The scales, the only inanimate object in the zodiac, are the symbol for Libra. You weigh things carefully, balancing one thing against another. And, just like a set of scales, you may swing wildly before you reach a point of equilibrium. The scales also symbolize judgement and justice. Libra is the skilled negotiator who brings harmony and conciliation. In fact, an earlier symbol for Libra was the dove, the peacemaker.

PERSONALITY

Charming and equable, you are easy-going and adaptable and enjoy leading your life in a laid-back style. You dislike direct confrontation and will do everything you can to keep the peace. Being "nice" is important to you, as is refinement and tastefulness. In fact, you try so often and so diligently to be nice and accommodating of other people's needs, that you may lose sight of yourself. When this happens, your own needs suddenly erupt with great force, surprising yourself and those around you.

Relationships mean a tremendous amount to you and you need people more than most signs. Because you hate arguments and separation, you will settle for any compromise as long as it allows you to stay with your partner. This may well mean being somewhat economical with the truth in order to maintain harmony. Libra is not beyond a little judicious juggling of the facts if it will preserve the facade of harmony.

Libra is known for having an indecisive personality. You weigh up all sides of an argument, and are able to see the value in each. This makes it difficult for you to choose and you sit on the fence for as long as you possibly can. Libra is an indolent sign. There is, however, an ambitious side to you that allows you to make an effort when required.

The dove, an old symbol for Libra, has your qualities of peacefulness and harmony.

APPEARANCE

Harmony is the keynote of the laid-back Libran appearance. You are drawn to colors that harmonize, fabrics that flow beautifully, and shapes that are pleasing to the eye. Your graceful body looks as though it was designed for pleasure. Your clothes represent the epitome of understated good taste. You rarely have a hair out of place, even when you are hurrying to keep an appointment for which you are very late – timekeeping is not one of Libra's strong points. Oozing charm, you will apologize graciously and be instantly forgiven. Who can resist such a beautiful being?

CAREER

Happiest working in partnership with others, Libra is the born diplomat, seeking the path of cooperation and conciliation. Any career that utilizes these qualities will be suitable. Counseling, marriage guidance, running a dating agency or management consultancy are ideal occupations.

Artistic and imaginative, you are interested in beauty in its many forms. Beautician, interior designer, art critic, designer of dresses or stage sets, artistic director or ballet dancer are all occupations that allow your talents to flow freely. The theater is your natural environment, but you also suit the world of law. You enjoy the cut and thrust of the courtroom, and the intrigue of negotiating behind the scenes.

Libra's need to see justice done often leads you into the courtroom or the conciliation service.

♏ | Scorpio

THE SCORPION

Intense and magnetic, Scorpio is one of the most passionate signs. You venture fearlessly into realms where others do not dare to tread. Your powerful mind and dominant personality make you difficult to ignore. Others find you enigmatic and mysterious: you value your privacy and do not reveal yourself easily. With an urge to master power and to push aside taboos, your instinctive understanding of the value of pain brings healing and new life.

THE SYMBOL

Scorpio has four symbols. First is the scorpion, whose nature is to sting itself to death. This is the characteristic of Scorpio that can be death-defying and destructive, but knows that death allows new growth. Second is the snake that sheds its skin – the transformation you are seeking. Third is the eagle that soars high above the ground, its all-seeing eye encompassing everything – but it pounces cruelly on its prey. Finally the phoenix, rising from the ashes, indicates the process of purification and rebirth that Scorpio undergoes.

PERSONALITY

The Scorpio personality is brooding and intense. Your insight, perspicacity, and sharp mind can penetrate to the heart of things. You are intuitive and empathetic and instinctively understand other people. But your sign is a secretive, enigmatic one: people find it hard to get to know you, and that suits you. You prefer to be the one who knows, rather than the one who is known.

You can be manipulative and compulsive, but you are also discerning and compassionate. Your healing power is strong. A loyal, fixed sign, you find it difficult to change and yet your aim is purification and transformation.

There is also a dark, destructive side to Scorpio. Instinctively you know that death is a necessary part of a process, but your entrenched thought patterns can become self-destructive. Jealousy and resentment are your shadow qualities, and you can hold a grudge forever.

Prince Charles epitomizes the enigmatic Scorpio aura of power. Everyone recognizes him, but few people are privy to his secrets.

APPEARANCE

Piercing eyes below well-defined brows dominate a hooked, hawklike nose – the profile is that of an eagle. The stance is self-assured and contained. You exude magnetism, mystery, and sex.

CAREER

As a Scorpio you enjoy careers that use your astute mind and ability to cut through to the heart of the matter – and your cunning ability to manipulate things to your advantage. Medicine (especially surgery), detection and law enforcement, finance, psychology, major corporations, and the armed forces all attract a Scorpio. Given Scorpio's link to elimination, sewage worker (or plumber) is an unusual but appropriate occupation. Less traditional careers are New Age psychics, practitioners of complementary medicine, and hospice work.

The occult fascinates Scorpios – who often use their hypnotic power as a healing tool.

Like your symbol, the Scorpion, you carry a powerful sting in your tail.

♐ | Sagittarius

Optimistic and open-minded, Sagittarius rides through life on an eternal quest. You ask the great questions of life: "What does it all mean?" and "What are we here for?" Enthusiastic and outgoing, you are always on the lookout for the next adventure, a fresh idea, or a new horizon. Your arrows shoot far and wide, but with little thought for where they land. Your devastating frankness can shock, but it is accompanied by integrity and good judgment.

THE SYMBOL

The archer epitomizes the Sagittarian spirit: bow raised to the sky, roaming free, looking to the far horizons, eternally seeking new targets. But the Sagittarian archer is the centaur, half man and half beast. This is the fusion of animal instincts with the rational mind – the point in the zodiac where you have to explain yourself and your world.

PERSONALITY

Engaged in an eternal search for meaning, yours is a freedom-loving sign. You fight for the right to believe as you will, and allow others their own beliefs, even though you are prone to proselytizing! Being tied down is anathema to you, and when bored you are positively lethal. If you cannot see any purpose in your life, then you may sink into depression and apathy, but your usual nature is jovial and expansive.

Your wide-ranging knowledge and intuitive understanding give you an innovative mind that usually has good judgement – although impulsiveness can lead you into trouble. You are a skillful initiator, but poor at following things through. With your low boredom

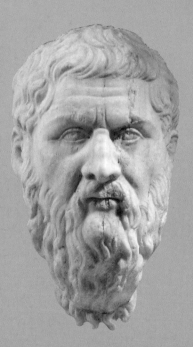

A natural philosopher, you shoot your arrows far and wide in your search for the meaning of life.

threshold, you leave it to others to carry out your ideas while you move on.

Sagittarius is a sign that values honesty and integrity. You are devastatingly frank and do not hesitate to offer an opinion, even when it has not been sought. Sagittarius is known for the tactless remark. For such a sociable sign, you make social blunders surprisingly often. But most people forgive you when they realize that you did not mean to cause offense.

Sagittarius suffers from the belief that the grass is always greener somewhere else. You may well inhabit a beautiful, Walter Mitty-like world of make-believe. Your powerful imagination may cause you to be restless and dissatisfied with life, unless you channel it to a good use.

Sagittarians make natural teachers. Your enquiring mind enjoys sharing knowledge with others – especially at the level of higher education.

APPEARANCE

Many Sagittarians have a sporty, athletic build, yet Sagittarius often trips, because this is a clumsy, uncoordinated sign. All Sagittarians have good legs and shapely ankles. Clothes are casual and informal. The distinguishing characteristic is a long, horsey face with a jovial expression.

CAREER

You enjoy sharing your knowledge, especially as a lecturer or a professor. Your philosophical bent takes you into the world of sociology, law, and publishing, and your flair for publicity opens doors in advertising.

Travel is your great love and a career in this field is ideal, as would be any activity in the leisure industry. Horses are strongly associated with your sign and may become a profession as well as a pleasure. You may have the ability to be a professional sportsman (or woman), but, if not, you could well find yourself employed in some way within a sports environment. Your versatility means that you may well follow more than one career – often finding yourself switching in mid-life.

♑ | # Capricorn

THE GOAT

Ambitious and tenacious, Capricorn has the drive to reach the top. You work determinedly to reach your goal, utilizing your innate discipline and ability to plan ahead. Once you have reached a position of authority, you are able to relax and explore your strong spiritual impulses. With a highly-developed sense of responsibility, you care deeply for society and uphold its conventions.

THE SYMBOL

Capricorn's symbol is the goat. Sometimes this may represent a domesticated goat, tied to a stake, reflecting the side of Capricorn that is chained to duty and responsibility. Then there is the mountain goat who progresses upward with sure-footed ease, seeming at times to defy gravity itself. The old symbol for Capricorn is the mythical sea-goat. This goat is not afraid of feelings but can rise above the instincts to consciousness of self.

PERSONALITY

Prudent, serious, and disciplined, as a Capricorn you have a strong sense of responsibility. You will strive to keep your own life in good order, especially financially. You are conventional with a high moral outlook. Indiscipline and chaos upset you, and you crave boundaries and organization in order to feel secure. You firmly believe in upholding society's rules.

Childhood may have been difficult for you. As a child you may have felt overwhelmed by the gap between the sense of duty, or the burden that you carried, and your ability to see this through. Capricorn has an old head on young shoulders, which gets progressively younger the more you mature. Old age allows your innate wisdom to shine through.

You belong to a receptive, negative sign. Negative signs are characterized as being inward-looking and softly focused. They are attuned to inner wisdom and open to spiritual guidance. This means that the rigid boundaries of "what should be" conflict with your need to grow spiritually. The old rules and regulations need to be freed so that you can direct your own life. A hard task, but one for which you are uniquely suited.

If you are unable to adapt, then the darker Capricorn qualities of rigidity, narrow-mindedness, and pessimism make themselves known. A deep air of

Take any group of influential people and you will be sure to find a hardworking Capricorn among them.

doom and gloom hangs over Capricorn, grimly holding onto what is known and safe. A contented Capricorn has good humor and great wit.

APPEARANCE

Capricorn is a bony sign. Long, lean, and appearing to be competent, you may become careworn if you do not achieve the success you seek. Many Capricorns look as though they are carrying a burden. Capricorn men often grow a beard, and in both sexes the hair has a tendency to turn gray early. In fact, there may be an overall gray tone to the skin and to clothing.

CAREER

Liking discipline and authority, you take up a career in local government or politics, the police, army, or the law. Concerned with structure and the fabric of society, you turn to architecture, property, and planning. With your deep connection to the past, geriatric care, antiques, and archaeology appeal, as does formal design. With your sign's link to the skeleton, osteopathy and chiropractic are suitable careers. Capricorns make excellent systems analysts, aides, directors, and personnel workers. When ambition is strong, you can be found in the highest positions in the land in both business and government.

In the most ancient of times, the Capricorn sea-goat rose from the waters of the unconscious to bring wisdom to the people of Mesopotamia.

♒ | Aquarius

THE WATER BEARER

Quirky, eccentric, and freedom-loving, individualistic Aquarius likes to be that little bit different. You have a remarkable ability to see into the future and identify the next trend. With a revolutionary spirit, you march to a different drum. Your idealism is strong and you have a deep desire to aid humanity.

THE SYMBOL

The water bearer is the symbol for Aquarius. This figure symbolizes rational consciousness pouring out the waters of life. A blend of intuition and reason, yours is a logical sign, prone to illogical behavior. Your task in life is to combine the two into a workable whole.

Rebellious Aquarius always stands out from the crowd. While not always as extreme as this young lady, people will notice you!

PERSONALITY

You were born ahead of your time and may well find it difficult to fit into conventional society. Aquarians clash with authority and have strong principles. Your rebellious nature finds it difficult to conform. With an ability to see farther ahead than most, you desire to change the world for the better.

Nevertheless, you have a huge conflict within you. Signs have "rulers" – planets with whom there is a special resonance. Aquarius has two rulers, which are the most contradictory and opposite planets possible! Chaotic and perverse, libertarian Uranus is a catalyst for change. This unpredictable planet signifies the rebel in your soul. Then there is conservative Saturn, which supports convention, morality, and the maintenance of the established order, and follows a rigid path. This is the aloof side of your nature that feels cut off from individual contact while maintaining its concern for the mass of humanity. The result is that you may be stuck in a rut, but a rut of the most unconventional kind. You set out on a course of behavior to be *different*, and find yourself trapped in thoughts and experiences that you no longer wish to follow but do not know how to change. Then Uranus comes along and boots you into something new.

This conflict reflects what you perceive in society. You want social justice for everyone and recognize that change is essential, but you find yourself fighting the very authority that could bring about that change. As an inventive Aquarian, you can become the instrument of reform – if you resolve your own inner conflict.

APPEARANCE

It is difficult to miss an unconventional Aquarian, because there is always something different about you. Whether it is your hippy style or way-out clothing, your latest hairstyle, or the static electricity crackling from your person, you stand out from the crowd. Aquarian men look wired – nervous and frenetic they operate at a very fast pace indeed.

CAREER

With your deep concern for social justice and changing conventional mores, you are found in occupations that aid humanity. Social and charity work, social policy, cutting-edge research science, medicine, psychiatry, electronics, and state-of-the art technology all appeal strongly, as does making the world a less polluted place. But so, too, does the unconventional appeal: astrology, vibrational medicine, punk rock, hypnotherapy – Aquarius tries them all.

You need a job that is provoking and challenging, one that engages your inventive mind and original thinking. Product research and development employs your inventor's skills and your ability to spot the next trend or see what will be needed in twenty years' time. Bringing about revolution of any kind satisfies your deepest cravings for something *different*.

With two opposite and opposing rulers, Aquarius is split between the conventional and the unconventional.

Pisces

THE FISHES

Dreamy and romantic, imaginative Pisces floats through life immersed in a world of subtle feelings and unconscious desires. You move to and fro in accordance with unseen emotional currents. Compassionate and impressionable, your concern for the welfare of others may lead you into victim or martyr scenarios. Your greatest desire is to find union with another and to merge back into the mystical oneness from which you came.

THE SYMBOL

The pair of fishes, swimming in opposite directions but joined in the middle, symbolize the dual nature of Pisces and the strong emotional currents that tug you in different directions. You have a desire for self-renunciation and yet vacillate wildly in your search for unconditional love.

PERSONALITY

You are one of the most emotional signs of the Zodiac, a creature of mood and whim. Artistic and visionary, you sometimes have trouble distinguishing between reality and the illusion created by your beautiful fantasies, which can lead to problems operating in the everyday world. Pisces tends to be vague and unfocused, especially when dealing with mundane matters.

Boundaries are a big issue for you. Kind and compassionate, and hating to say no, you tend to give yourself away too easily. People make demands on your sympathy and you feel you must help, whatever the personal cost. If you do not, you fall into guilt. Taking on too much and, hating to disappoint anyone, you spread yourself too thinly. Confused, you slide away, only to swim back at another time. This elusive quality, and your tendency to be sidetracked, make it difficult for other people to know where they stand with you. Your intentions are good, but your will is weak, and with your escapist urges, that can lead you into trouble.

APPEARANCE

Your eyes are your most striking feature. They are dreamer's eyes – deep, melting, and compassionate, they are eyes to drown in. Your eyes look beyond and into another world.

Soft, melting, and oh so deep, Pisces' eyes hypnotize, drowning you in their depths.

CAREER

Caring and empathetic, you seek employment where you feel needed. While you do not like discipline, nursing and medicine express your compassionate nature. Counseling and other helping professions, especially working with drug or alcohol problems, also give you scope to express your sympathetic nature and your need to be a savior. However, difficulty over boundaries and the tendency be sucked into people's problems lead to victim or martyr situations. Remember that expressing sympathy takes you into the problems, while empathy allows you to detach and see what can be done. As Pisces rules the feet, chiropody, podiatry, or footwear design are appropriate careers.

The world of movies and make-believe reflects Pisces' vivid imagination.

You have great artistic talent and a boundless imagination so the arts provide an excellent place for you to express yourself, as an actor, dancer, writer, painter, poet, or illusionist, or animator, photographer or computer artist – you can explore them all in the quest to fulfill your talents.

With your hypnotic quality and psychic abilities, you may also want to try your skills at being a hypnotist, channeler (or psychic artist), Tarot reader, or intuitive healer.

The Elements

Water, earth, air, and fire: the elements of the emotions, the body, the mind, and the intuition.

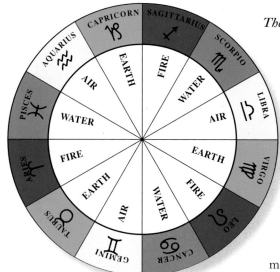

The zodiac wheel is an orderly pattern of elemental forces – a kaleidoscope of color. Signs which share the same color harmonize and attract. Other colors may be pulled in – or be repelled by a different perspective on life.

The astrological Elements – earth, water, air, and fire, are related to different ways of being and to our perception of the world. Earth relates to the physical function, water to the emotions, air to the intellect, and fire to the spirit or intuition. The zodiac is divided into three sets of signs of each element, which have special affinity with each other. The elements regulate the action of planets placed within them.

How strong an element will be depends on your personal birthchart. Your Sun-sign personality is powerfully motivated by the element in which the Sun is placed. You may, however, have several of the planets in a different element, enhancing that element with greater strength. This book will show you which element your Sun, Moon, Ascendant, Neptune, and Pluto are placed in. People who share the same element tend to understand each other very well, and to be attracted to their fellow signs. This is not at all surprising, since they share a mutual approach to life. People who come from a very different elemental balance find it hard to understand each other – earth puts out fire, for instance, as does water while air fans the flames

EARTH
Taurus, Virgo, and Capricorn

Related to the practical and sensation level of being, earth signs are pragmatic and grounded – literally, "down-to-earth." Self-sufficient earth's concerns are to do with survival and security. This is the most productive of the elements, and is known for shaping matter into physical form. Earth signs utilize the five senses of taste, touch, smell, sight, and hearing in order to understand the practical world around them. It is also a sensual element – earth-sign people are at home in their bodies.

WATER
Cancer, Scorpio, and Pisces

Linked to sensitivity, feeling, and perception, the water signs are emotional and imaginative. This is a passive, rhythmic element that ebbs and flows.

Water people have a desire to look inward, and need to take time to process their emotions. Motivation is unconscious, concerned with subtle feelings and emotional needs. Attuned to delicate nuances, the water signs are empathetic and caring. This is an element that has a deep craving for other people, experiencing itself most strongly through an interchange of feelings.

AIR

Gemini, Libra, and Aquarius

Intellectual and innovative, air signs are ideas people, who see new and infinite possibilities. This is the communicative element that works through self-expression and mental concepts. Air signs need other people for an exchange of ideas. To them, discussion is more important than food. Mutual understanding is absolutely essential for this connective element and mental rapport is essential in an air relationship.

FIRE

Aries, Leo, and Sagittarius

Active and out-going, the fire element is an encapsulation of the creative urge. It brings new possibilities into being. Fire signs possess an enormous appetite for life. This element ranges widely in the search for inspiration and vision. It is an element that operates in the realm of spirit and intuition. True creation is the act of the visionary fire element. Too much fire in a chart can lead to burnout, but without fire there would be no regeneration, no creative spark.

The Qualities

The Qualities describe how the energy of a chart will flow: whether it will move determinedly, initiating as it goes (cardinal); whether it will be stuck in a rigid channel (fixed); or whether it will flow easily and adaptively (mutable). Signs that share the same Quality tend to have the same approach to life – assertive, cautious, or flexible.

The Qualities describe your relationship to the environment and indicate how you handle life. Cardinal signs like to be in control and to initiate changes in the environment. Fixed signs like control, but as long as your environment remains stable, you are more interested in personal matters and you dislike change. Mutable signs are flexible and you adapt to the environment.

QUALITIES, ELEMENTS, AND PLANETS

Each element has one cardinal sign, one fixed, and one mutable. This subtly directs how the elemental energy flows, whether it can move directly or meets blockages, and whether it can adapt to change, or resists.

Of the planets, the qualities most strongly affect the Sun. Cardinal placement means that the Sun is the most active of that element. A fixed Sun is the most rigid and a mutable Sun the most flexible expression. Nevertheless, qualities affect all planets. Planets can show their nature more directly in cardinal signs. In fixed signs the more intractable side of a planet shows itself. In adaptable mutable signs, the planet finds its natural mode of expression. Several planets in one quality may well overrule the Sun in a different quality.

CARDINAL
Aries, Cancer, Libra, and Capricorn
Active, outgoing, and enterprising, cardinal signs want to make their mark on the world. This quality gets things moving, initiates, and urges. You want to control things, especially your environment. You are ambitious, even though

Cardinal signs go straight to the point.

Fixed signs are rigid and unmoving.

Mutable signs flow freely.

you may tend to hide this. Assertive and strong-willed, you enjoy challenge and meet this head on in the case of Aries and Capricorn, less directly with Libra, and sideways on with Cancer. But the underlying urge to assert yourself is still there – it simply manifests in subtler ways.

FIXED
Taurus, Leo, Scorpio, and Aquarius
Resistant to change and resenting outside influences, fixed signs prefer a stable life and an orderly routine. You are the most reliable of the qualities, steadfastly carrying things through. This is the most loyal element. Deeply entrenched, you want your life to be predictable and you find yourself feeling profoundly uncomfortable when presented with the need to alter the status quo.

MUTABLE
Gemini, Virgo, Sagittarius, and Pisces
Flexible and adaptable, mutable signs enjoy change. Yours is the most unpredictable lifestyle and you like the instability. You are versatile and enthusiastic, always meeting new situations as they arise. You hate routine and are easily bored, so you welcome outside influences that stimulate and intrigue.

The mutable signs enjoy a flexible, changing environment while the fixed signs prefer stable, controled certainty. Cardinal signs create their own ambience.

The Polarities

The signs of the zodiac are split into two polarities: positive and negative, which alternate around the zodiac wheel. The terms refer to how the energies of the zodiac are used. Positive signs are outgoing and active; negative signs are receptive and inward-looking. The two polarities are complementary to each other – neither is better or worse than the other.

Zodiac wheel showing the polarities.

THE YIN AND YANG OF THE CHART

The terms "positive" and "negative" are not judgmental. "Masculine" and "feminine" are also used to describe the two different ways of using the zodiac energies. They are the yin and the yang of the chart. One energy flows outward, while the other flows inward. The energies are complementary to each other and both are needed for a balanced flow of energy.

The overall balance of the planets placed in positive and negative signs is important. If an element is overemphasized by several planets placed in the opposite polarity to the Sun, then a passive and introverted Sun is rendered more exuberant; or an active, extroverted Sun is calmed and quietened. Certain planets are more comfortable in negative signs – the Moon and Neptune for instance – while others find the positive signs more compatible – Mars for example. If a planet is in an incompatible polarity, then the free flow of energy is blocked and may become self-destructive or overly rebellious, creating problems.

Positive signs
Aries, Gemini, Leo, Libra, Sagittarius, and Aquarius
The positive signs of the zodiac are active, extroverted, and self-expressive. You are outer-directed, or orientated to the exterior world. The positive energy sets things in motion. Fire and air element signs are positive.

Negative signs
Taurus, Cancer, Virgo, Scorpio, Capricorn, and Pisces
The negative signs of the zodiac are receptive, reflective, self-repressive, and introverted. You are inward-directed, or orientated to the inner world. You are compliant and acquiescent. Water and earth element signs are negative.

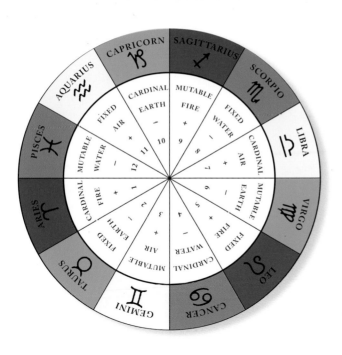

Subtle Differences

Each of the zodiac signs is a complex mix of the Element, the Quality and the Polarity. This is what makes each sign unique. Each combination reflects subtle differences in energy flow, direction, self expression and self-awareness.

♈ *Aries: Positive Cardinal Fire*
Go-getting Aries is the most dynamic expression of assertive positive fire. The enterprising and impetuous cardinal quality urges you onward.

♉ *Taurus: Negative Fixed Earth*
Taurus is the intransigent expression of negative earth. This cautious fixed quality may lock you into a rigid routine.

♊ *Gemini: Positive Mutable Air*
Versatile Gemini is the most adaptable expression of positive air. The flexible mutable quality helps you to adjust to any situation.

♋ *Cancer: Negative Cardinal Water*
Cancer is the most tenacious expression of negative water. The ambitious cardinal quality, however, impels you forward.

♌ *Leo: Positive Fixed Fire*
The most inflexible of the positive fire signs, your fixed quality restrains the usual impetuosity of fire.

♍ *Virgo: Negative Mutable Earth*
The most flexible of the earth signs, the adaptable mutable quality imparts versatility and adroitness to the ponderous earth element.

♎ *Libra: Positive Cardinal Air*
Positive air is a lively energy, but not one noted necessarily for personal drive. The cardinal quality kickstarts you into action.

♏ *Scorpio: Negative Fixed Water*
The most intractable of the negative water signs, the fixed quality imparts an added stubbornness to the usually acquiescent water element.

♐ *Sagittarius: Positive Mutable Fire*
The adaptable mutable quality imparts even more verve to the positive fire element. You are the most restless and unfocused of the fire signs.

♑ *Capricorn: Negative Cardinal Earth*
By far the most ambitious of the negative earth signs, the cardinal quality adds a drive that is usually lacking in this receptive element.

♒ *Aquarius: Positive Fixed Air*
The fixed quality imparts an inflexibility not normally found in positive air signs, but makes for disciplined and well-organized thought.

♓ *Pisces: Negative Mutable Water*
The mutable quality emphasizes your tendency to react fluidly to each and every stimulus.

The Planets

An important part of the horoscope, the planets represent principles and drives within the psyche. They are like archetypes, or universal symbols. The planets also appear in the outer environment, and while they themselves do not actually cause anything to happen, it feels that way to us. Every planet has a specific meaning, undertakes a certain function, and behaves in a typical way.

Each of the planets has its own unique orbit – which in astrological terms appears to travel around the earth rather than the Sun.

A UNIQUE PATTERN

The distribution of the planets in your birthchart is a unique pattern based on the moment of your birth. Only someone born on the same day, in the same place, and at the same time as you shares your chart.

Planets function in a particular sign in accordance with the energetic impulses of that sign. Once you understand how the planets function, you have a deep insight into the psyche.

According to metaphysical law, we resonate to the movement of the planets and their ever-changing complex interweaving through the sky. Not such a surprising thought when you realize that the Moon not only controls the tides but can also affect shellfish deep within the oceans. The day-to-day movements of the planets appear to act as triggers or catalysts for events (often referred to in newspaper and magazine horoscopes), but they represent drives deep within us that are currently finding an outlet.

PLANETARY ORDER

Astrology uses the planets as seen from the perspective of the Earth. The planets that are "closest" to the Earth and move quickly are the ones that can manifest most consciously and are known as "personal" planets. These planets are visible to the naked eye. The outer planets, known as "transpersonal" planets, take longer to move around the chart and represent much longer-term influences.

Gemini	Mercury	Virgo
Taurus	Venus	Libra
Aries	Mars	Scorpio *plus Pluto*
plus Neptune Pisces	Jupiter	Sagittarius
plus Uranus Aquarius	Saturn	Capricorn

Cancer – Moon   Leo – Sun

NEW DISCOVERIES

When a new planet is discovered it brings that energy into consciousness. Pluto saw the birth of nuclear power, with its enormous untold potential for destruction, but also its possible applications in medicine and the production of energy. It coincided with deeper exploration of the human psyche.

It is not only planets far out in the solar system that await discovery. In 1977 Chiron (actually a "dead" comet but adopted by astrologers as a "planet") signified an increasing interest in complementary medicine, shamanism, and psychotherapy, bringing together shattered parts of the psyche.

PLANETARY RULERS

Certain planets have a special affinity with particular signs. In traditional astrology the seven planets visible to the naked eye were known as "rulers." The more recently discovered planets have also been allotted to signs because they were seen as being more in accord with the planetary energies, although the effects of the traditional rulers can still be ascertained.

PLANETARY MOVEMENT

Not all the planets pass through signs uniformly. Planets like Uranus, Pluto, and Chiron have eccentric orbits that move through some signs relatively quickly and through others extremely slowly.

Approximate time taken for each planet to move around a birthchart

The Sun	1 year	*Saturn*	29 years
The Moon	28 days	*Chiron*	50–51 years
Mercury	1 year	*Uranus*	84 years
Venus	1 year	*Neptune*	165 years
Mars	2 years	*Pluto*	248 years
Jupiter	12 years		

Planets

Sun ☉

Moon ☽

Mercury ☿

Venus ♀

Mars ♂

Jupiter ♃

Saturn ♄

Chiron ⚷

Uranus ♅

Neptune ♆

Pluto ♇

North Node ☊

The Moon

The Moon is concerned with feelings, emotion, and mothering. It is fluctuating, cyclical, and receptive. It shows our instincts and habitual patterns; our heredity and our reproductive urges. It describes what we need in order to feel nurtured and secure. The Moon also illuminates the emotional baggage we carry. This is the fastest-moving planet, spending only two and a half days in a sign.

The Moon travels around the zodiac in less than a month, subtly coloring your Sun-sign. In the birthchart, this is what helps to make you your own unique self. You respond at a feeling and emotional level from your Moon. The Moon also has a day-to-day effect. With an elliptical, fluctuating orbit, it moves slightly faster through some signs than others. Each month the Moon gently pulls you in a cyclical, rhythmic flow in accord with this cycle.

DEEPEST NEEDS

When you understand the irrational Moon, you understand your deepest feelings and motivation. The Moon shows what you need to make you feel secure. For this reason, it may have a deeper influence on your behavior than your Sun-sign. If your Moon is in a deeply emotional sign, it can overcome the most rigidly controlled Sun- signs. If it is in a deeply repressed sign, your emotions will be blocked and unable to flow. In a moody, Moon-orientated sign like Cancer or Pisces, unrecognized feelings will create irrational emotional outbursts in the coldest of signs.

THE INSTINCTUAL MOON

The Moon is receptive and passive. It reflects our experience, rather than initiating it. The energies of the Moon operate from the subconscious mind: it is our instincts and our autonomous body processes. This is where we make an automatic reaction to a programed response. In karmic astrology, the Moon shows patterns of behavior and powerful emotional responses that were laid down in other lifetimes.

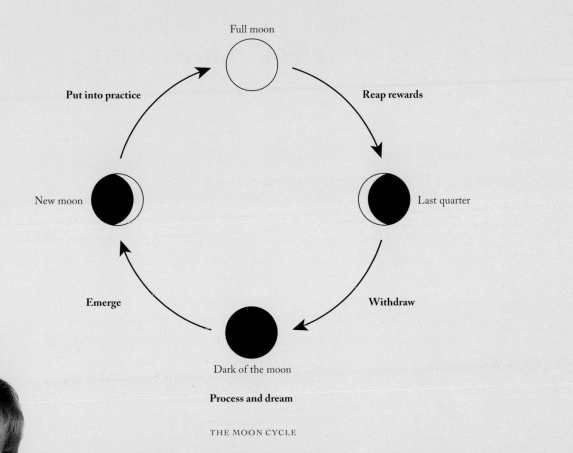

Full moon

Put into practice

Reap rewards

New moon

Last quarter

Emerge

Withdraw

Dark of the moon

Process and dream

THE MOON CYCLE

THE MOON AND THE MOTHER

The Moon is about mothering style. No matter what Sun-sign your mother was born under, the Moon describes your expectations and experience of being mothered. The Moon also describes the kind of nurturing you seek and your maternal instincts. Some signs are deeply maternal, others need mothering but have little time for nurturing others. Your Moon placement shows the "lunar food" you crave to feed your deepest need. The Moon is habits laid down in early childhood and what we inherit from our families.

THE MOON CYCLE

The Moon affects all human experience. The dark of the Moon allows you to withdraw, process your feelings, and dream. Then, with the new Moon, you return to the world and put the insights you have gained during your period of withdrawal into practice. As the Moon comes to full, you will find yourself reaping the rewards of your efforts. Then, with the old Moon you withdraw into a period of contemplation once again.

☽ | Finding your Moon Sign

Days of the Moon

Day	Signs	Degrees
1	0	–
2	1	13
3	1	26
4	1–2	39
5	2	52
6	2	65
7	3	78
8	3	91
9	4	104
10	4	117
11	5	130
12	5	143
13	5–6	156
14	6	169
15	6	182
16	7	195
17	7	208
18	8	221
19	8	234
20	9	247
21	9	260
22	10	273
23	10	286
24	10–11	299
25	11	312
26	11	325
27	12	338
28	12	351
29	1	364
30	1	377
31	2	390

The Moon Tables on the following pages set out the positions of the Moon at noon Greenwich Mean Time (GMT) on the first day of the month. This is equivalent to 7.00 am Eastern Standard Time (EST) and 4.00 am Pacific Standard Time (PST). It is 1.00 pm British Summer Time (BST). In Western Australia it would be 8.00 pm, in the East 10.00 pm, and in New Zealand, midnight.

The Moon changes signs every two and a half days or so, and moves around the zodiac in 28–9 days. (There are 30° in each Zodiac sign; see the wheel for the order of the signs.) If you have a natal chart, this will give the position of your Moon. If you do not have a chart, an astrologer or a computer will accurately calculate the position of your Moon, but you can work out a rough position using the Moon Tables that follow. With a little more calculation you can find a somewhat more accurate position.

To find the rough position of your Moon
• Find the position of the Moon on the first day of your birth month and year using the Moon Tables overleaf.
• Using the Days of the Moon Table, find your day of birth.
• Under "signs," you will find the approximate number of signs of the zodiac that you need to count forward from the first of the month to midday on your birthday. This will give you an approximate Moon placement, but it can be out by a sign either side – in which case read the descriptions of the Moons on either side to see which feels right to you.
So, for example, if you were born on the 18th day of the month, you will need to move forward eight signs on the zodiac wheel. If the Moon is in Capricorn on the first of the month, this will take you to Virgo.

To find a more accurate Moon position
• Find the position of the Moon on the first day of your birth month and year using the Moon Tables overleaf.
• Find your day of birth on the Days of the Moon Table.
• Add the number of degrees shown in the "degrees" column of the Days of the Moon Table to the Moon's position on the first of your birthday month

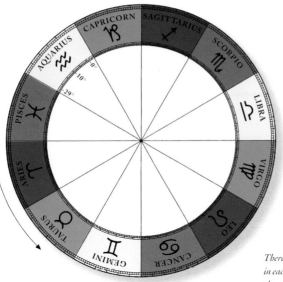

*There are 30 degrees
in each sign around
the zodiac wheel.*

in the Moon Tables. (Use the zodiac wheel to help you, remembering that one sign is 30°, two signs 60°, three signs 90°, and so on.)

• Calculate your GMT time of birth. (See page 92 for US time zones and the UK and USA Summertime adjustments).

• The Moon moves approximately one degree every two hours. If you were born before noon GMT, subtract half a degree for each hour separating your time of birth from noon. If you were born after noon, add half a degree for each hour until your time of birth. So, for example, if you were born at 6.00 am GMT (or its equivalent) and the table for your day of birth showed the Moon at 15° ♈ (Aries), you would subtract 3°, giving you a Moon placement of 12° Aries. If you were born at 6.00 pm, then the placement would be 18° Aries.

If you do not have a birthdate

If you do not know your time of birth, calculate for noon. Check whether the Moon could have changed signs during the day (Is it within 6° of the end or beginning of a sign?) If it could have, read the interpretation for the other sign. You will know from the description of the signs which is right for you.

*Diana was the goddess of the
Moon in Roman mythology.*

☽ | Moon Tables

♈ Aries	♎ Libra
♉ Taurus	♏ Scorpio
♊ Gemini	♐ Sagittarius
♋ Cancer	♑ Capricorn
♌ Leo	♒ Aquarius
♍ Virgo	♓ Pisces

	Jan	Feb	Mar	Apr	May	Jun	Jul	Aug	Sep	Oct	Nov	Dec
1920	9°♉	2°♋	26°♋	17°♍	22°♎	8°♐	10°♑	26°♒	14°♈	21°♉	14°♋	23°♌
1921	14°♎	0°♐	9°♐	23°♑	25°♎	9°♈	14°♉	5°♋	29°♌	7°♎	27°♏	1°♑
1922	16°♒	0°♈	9°♈	25°♉	1°♋	23°♌	2°♎	25°♏	14°♑	18°♒	2°♈	4°♉
1923	20°♊	9°♌	17°♌	10°♎	18°♏	11°♐	16°♒	1°♈	15°♉	17°♊	3°♌	9°♍
1924	0°♏	24°♐	19°♑	9°♓	13°♈	28°♉	1°♋	16°♌	5°♎	13°♏	6°♑	15°♒
1925	4°♈	21°♉	29°♉	12°♋	14°♌	29°♍	4°♏	26°♐	20°♒	28°♓	18°♉	22°♊
1926	6°♌	20°♍	29°♍	16°♏	23°♐	15°♒	25°♓	17°♉	5°♋	8°♌	22°♍	24°♎
1927	10°♐	29°♑	7°♒	0°♈	8°♉	1°♋	6°♌	21°♍	5°♏	8°♐	24°♑	0°♓
1928	23°♈	16°♊	10°♋	0°♍	4°♎	18°♏	21°♐	7°♒	26°♓	4°♉	28°♊	6°♌
1929	27°♍	11°♏	18°♏	2°♑	4°♒	20°♓	25°♈	17°♊	11°♌	19°♍	8°♏	12°♐
1930	26°♑	11°♓	24°♓	7°♉	14°♊	8°♌	17°♍	8°♏	25°♐	28°♑	12°♓	14°♈
1931	0°♊	20°♋	28°♋	21°♍	0°♏	21°♐	26°♑	11°♓	25°♈	28°♉	15°♋	22°♌
1932	15°♎	8°♐	2°♑	21°♒	24°♈	8°♉	11°♊	27°♋	17°♍	25°♎	19°♐	27°♑
1933	15°♓	0°♉	8°♉	22°♊	24°♋	10°♍	16°♎	9°♐	2°♒	10°♓	29°♈	2°♊
1934	17°♋	2°♍	10°♍	29°♎	6°♐	0°♒	8°♓	29°♈	16°♊	18°♋	1°♍	3°♎
1935	20°♏	11°♑	19°♑	12°♓	21°♈	12°♊	16°♋	1°♍	16°♎	19°♏	7°♑	14°♒
1936	8°♈	0°♊	24°♊	11°♌	14°♍	28°♎	1°♐	17°♑	8°♓	17°♈	10°♊	17°♋
1937	5°♍	20°♎	28°♎	12°♐	14°♑	1°♓	8°♈	1°♊	24°♋	1°♍	19°♎	23°♏
1938	7°♑	22°♒	1°♓	20°♈	27°♉	21°♋	29°♌	19°♎	5°♐	7°♑	21°♒	23°♓
1939	10°♉	1°♋	10°♋	4°♍	12°♎	2°♐	6°♑	21°♒	6°♈	10°♉	29°♊	7°♌

	Jan	Feb	Mar	Apr	May	Jun	Jul	Aug	Sep	Oct	Nov	Dec
1940	0°♎	22°♏	15°♐	2°♒	4°♓	18°♈	20°♉	8°♋	29°♌	7°♎	1°♐	7°♑
1941	25°♒	9°♈	17°♈	1°♊	5°♋	23°♌	0°♎	23°♏	16°♑	23°♒	10°♈	13°♉
1942	27°♊	13°♌	21°♌	10°♎	18°♏	12°♑	20°♒	9°♈	25°♉	27°♊	11°♌	13°♍
1943	1°♏	23°♐	2°♑	26°♒	4°♈	23°♉	27°♊	11°♌	26°♍	1°♏	20°♐	29°♑
1944	22°♓	14°♉	6°♊	22°♋	24°♌	8°♎	10°♏	28°♐	19°♒	28°♓	21°♉	28°♊
1945	15°♌	29°♍	7°♎	22°♏	26°♐	14°♒	22°♓	16°♉	8°♋	14°♌	0°♎	3°♏
1946	17°♐	3°♒	11°♒	1°♈	9°♉	3°♋	10°♌	29°♍	15°♏	16°♐	0°♒	3°♓
1947	22°♈	14°♊	24°♊	16°♌	25°♍	14°♏	17°♐	2°♒	17°♓	22°♈	12°♊	21°♋
1948	14°♍	5°♏	26°♏	12°♑	14°♒	28°♓	0°♉	18°♊	10°♌	19°♍	12°♏	18°♐
1949	5°♒	19°♓	28°♓	12°♉	16°♊	6°♌	15°♍	8°♏	29°♐	5°♒	21°♓	23°♈
1950	7°♊	24°♋	1°♌	22°♍	0°♏	24°♐	1°♒	19°♓	4°♉	6°♊	21°♋	24°♌
1951	13°♎	6°♐	17°♐	10°♒	17°♓	4°♉	8°♊	22°♋	7°♍	12°♎	4°♐	12°♑
1952	5°♓	25°♈	16°♉	2°♋	3°♌	17°♍	20°♎	9°♐	1°♒	10°♓	2°♉	8°♊
1953	25°♋	9°♍	18°♍	3°♏	8°♐	26°♑	7°♓	0°♉	21°♊	26°♋	11°♍	13°♎
1954	27°♏	14°♑	21°♑	12°♓	21°♈	15°♊	21°♋	9°♍	24°♎	26°♏	11°♑	15°♒
1955	5°♈	28°♉	9°♊	2°♌	8°♍	25°♎	28°♏	12°♑	28°♒	3°♈	25°♉	3°♋
1956	26°♌	16°♎	7°♏	21°♐	23°♑	7°♓	11°♈	0°♊	23°♋	2°♍	24°♎	29°♏
1957	15°♑	29°♒	8°♓	24°♈	29°♉	20°♋	29°♌	22°♎	12°♐	16°♑	1°♓	2°♈
1958	17°♉	4°♋	12°♋	3°♍	12°♎	5°♐	12°♑	29°♒	14°♈	16°♉	1°♋	7°♌
1959	28°♍	21°♏	2°♐	24°♑	0°♓	15°♈	18°♉	2°♋	18°♌	24°♍	16°♏	24°♐
1960	17°♒	6°♈	26°♈	11°♊	13°♋	27°♌	1°♎	21°♏	15°♑	23°♒	14°♈	20°♉
1961	5°♋	20°♌	28°♌	14°♎	19°♏	11°♑	20°♒	13°♈	3°♊	7°♋	21°♌	22°♍
1962	6°♏	24°♐	3°♑	24°♒	3°♈	28°♉	3°♋	19°♌	4°♎	7°♏	23°♐	28°♑
1963	20°♓	13°♉	24°♉	15°♋	20°♌	5°♎	8°♏	22°♐	8°♒	14°♓	7°♉	15°♊
1964	7°♌	26°♍	16°♎	1°♐	3°♑	18°♒	22°♓	13°♉	6°♋	15°♌	6°♎	11°♏
1965	26°♐	10°♒	18°♒	5°♈	10°♉	3°♋	11°♌	4°♎	23°♏	26°♐	10°♒	12°♓
1966	26°♈	14°♊	23°♊	16°♌	25°♍	17°♏	23°♐	10°♒	24°♓	27°♈	14°♊	20°♋
1967	12°♍	6°♏	16°♏	6°♑	11°♒	25°♓	27°♈	11°♊	28°♋	5°♍	27°♎	6°♐
1968	28°♑	16°♓	6°♈	20°♉	23°♊	8°♌	14°♍	5°♏	28°♐	7°♒	27°♓	1°♉
1969	16°♊	0°♌	9°♌	25°♍	1°♏	24°♐	3°♒	25°♓	13°♉	16°♊	0°♌	1°♍

	Jan	Feb	Mar	Apr	May	Jun	Jul	Aug	Sep	Oct	Nov	Dec
1970	17°♎	5°♐	15°♐	8°♒	17°♓	8°♉	14°♊	0°♌	14°♍	17°♎	5°♐	12°♑
1971	4°♓	27°♈	7°♉	27°♊	1°♌	15°♍	17°♎	1°♐	18°♉	25°♒	18°♈	27°♉
1972	18°♋	5°♍	26°♍	10°♏	13°♐	29°♑	5°♓	28°♈	21°♊	29°♋	18°♍	22°♎
1973	6°♐	20°♑	28°♑	15°♓	22°♈	15°♊	23°♋	15°♍	3°♏	6°♐	19°♑	21°♒
1974	7°♈	27°♉	9°♊	0°♌	9°♍	0°♏	5°♐	20°♑	5°♓	8°♈	26°♉	3°♋
1975	26°♌	19°♎	28°♎	17°♐	21°♑	5°♓	6°♈	21°♉	9°♋	16°♌	9°♎	18°♏
1976	8°♑	25°♒	16°♓	1°♉	3°♊	20°♋	27°♌	20°♎	13°♐	21°♑	9°♓	12°♈
1977	26°♉	10°♋	18°♋	0°♍	12°♎	5°♐	14°♑	6°♓	23°♈	25°♉	9°♋	12°♌
1978	28°♍	18°♏	29°♏	22°♑	1°♓	21°♈	26°♉	18°♋	25°♌	28°♍	17°♏	24°♐
1979	18°♒	10°♈	18°♈	7°♊	10°♋	24°♌	26°♍	11°♏	0°♑	7°♒	1°♈	9°♉
1980	29°♊	16°♌	6°♍	21°♎	24°♏	12°♑	19°♒	12°♈	5°♊	12°♋	29°♌	2°♎
1981	16°♏	0°♑	8°♑	26°♒	3°♈	26°♉	5°♋	26°♌	13°♎	15°♏	29°♐	2°♒
1982	19°♓	10°♉	21°♉	15°♋	23°♌	12°♎	16°♏	1°♑	15°♒	18°♓	8°♉	15°♊
1983	9°♌	1°♎	9°♎	27°♏	0°♑	14°♏	16°♓	2°♉	21°♊	29°♋	23°♍	1°♏
1984	20°♐	6°♒	27°♒	11°♈	15°♉	3°♋	11°♌	4°♎	27°♍	3°♑	20°♒	22°♓
1985	5°♉	20°♊	28°♊	16°♌	24°♍	17°♏	26°♐	16°♒	3°♈	5°♉	19°♊	23°♋
1986	11°♍	3°♏	14°♏	7°♑	15°♒	3°♈	7°♉	21°♊	5°♌	9°♍	28°♎	6°♐
1987	0°♒	21°♓	29°♓	17°♉	20°♊	4°♌	6°♍	22°♎	12°♐	21°♑	15°♓	22°♈
1988	11°♊	26°♋	17°♌	1°♎	5°♏	24°♐	2°♒	26°♓	18°♉	24°♊	10°♌	11°♍
1989	25°♎	10°♐	18°♐	7°♒	15°♓	9°♉	17°♊	7°♌	23°♍	25°♎	10°♐	14°♑
1990	3°♓	25°♈	8°♉	29°♊	6°♌	24°♍	27°♎	10°♐	25°♑	29°♒	19°♈	27°♉
1991	20°♋	11°♍	19°♍	7°♏	10°♐	24°♑	27°♒	14°♈	5°♊	14°♋	7°♍	14°♎
1992	2°♐	17°♑	7°♒	22°♓	28°♈	15°♊	23°♋	17°♍	9°♏	14°♐	29°♑	1°♓
1993	14°♈	0°♊	9°♊	28°♋	7°♍	0°♏	8°♐	27°♑	13°♓	16°♈	0°♊	8°♋
1994	25°♌	18°♎	28°♎	20°♐	27°♑	14°♓	16°♈	0°♊	15°♋	19°♌	9°♎	17°♏
1995	11°♑	2°♓	10°♓	27°♈	0°♊	14°♋	14°♌	5°♎	27°♍	8°♑	29°♒	6°♈
1996	22°♉	7°♊	27°♋	12°♍	16°♎	6°♐	14°♑	8°♓	29°♈	4°♊	19°♋	21°♌
1997	4°♎	20°♏	29°♏	20°♑	29°♒	22°♈	0°♊	18°♋	3°♍	8°♎	21°♏	26°♐
1998	17°♒	10°♈	19°♈	12°♊	18°♋	4°♍	8°♎	20°♏	5°♑	9°♒	0°♈	8°♉
1999	2°♋	22°♌	1°♍	17°♎	20°♏	4°♑	8°♒	27°♓	19°♉	29°♊	21°♌	27°♍

	Jan	Feb	Mar	Apr	May	Jun	Jul	Aug	Sep	Oct	Nov	Dec
2000	13°♏	27°♐	17°♑	2°♓	29°♓	27°♉	5°♋	29°♌	19°♎	24°♏	8°♑	10°♒
2001	24°♓	11°♊	20°♉	12°♋	21°♌	14°♎	22°♏	8°♑	23°♒	26°♈	11°♉	16°♊
2002	7°♌	1°♎	9°♎	2°♐	7°♑	23°♒	26°♓	9°♉	24°♊	29°♋	21°♍	0°♏
2003	22°♐	12°♒	21°♒	7°♈	10°♉	25°♊	29°♋	19°♍	11°♏	21°♐	12°♒	17°♓
2004	2°♉	17°♊	6°♋	22°♌	26°♍	17°♏	25°♐	19°♒	10°♈	14°♉	28°♊	29°♋
2005	15°♍	6°♏	12°♏	3°♑	14°♒	6°♈	13°♉	29°♊	14°♌	16°♍	1°♏	7°♐

*The Moon cycle influences
the way we feel and behave.*

The Moon in Aries, Taurus, Gemini, Cancer

With the Moon in Taurus, your greatest fear is to meet "the Great No-Sayer," an overpowering mother figure who controls your life.

THE MOON IN ARIES

Your emotions are headstrong and tempestuous, and your instincts overwhelming. Your needs are powerful and demand instant gratification. You cannot tolerate frustration. A part of your psyche is like a young child. This Moon can often be self-centered and insensitive to other people's needs, concerned only with self-gratification. When your Moon has matured, you are capable of deep concern for others, and will fight for their rights if necessary.

LUNAR FOOD You crave admiration and validation. Without this, you sulk and wither. With it, you show your warm-hearted generosity of spirit.

MOTHER You seek ego-building, confident support from a mother who encourages your independent nature. What you may experience is a powerful figure, egotistical and self-centered; someone who puts her own needs first.

THE MOON IN TAURUS

Your overwhelming need is for security. You value your home and your family, possessively holding on to what you have. With fixed habits and firm control, you are prepared to make emotional sacrifices to stay safe. Nevertheless, you appreciate a comfortable lifestyle and may indulge yourself. Your emotional expression may be inhibited but your sex drive is strong. Once you are in a relationship, you stick with it no matter what. This is a jealous Moon.

LUNAR FOOD You desire a comfortable and secure life that offers you plenty of affection. If you do not have this, you may take refuge in habits such as comfort eating and addictions.

MOTHER You seek a dependable mother, one who gives you the ordered routine you crave. The safe, secure home is what makes you feel loved. What you may experience is a possessive, overpowering "No-sayer" who controls your life.

THE MOON IN GEMINI

Your great need is to be heard. You may fear and refuse to feel your emotions, from which you are isolated. Your tendency is to rationalize your feelings and you have little time for emotional displays from others. Your instinct is to be emotionally uncommitted. Yours is a fickle, changeable Moon. Its cunning and guile does not hesitate to manipulate the feelings of others.

LUNAR FOOD You crave mental stimulation and attention, which you use as a substitute for emotional satisfaction.

MOTHER You seek a mother who is communicative and who enters into your mental world. What you may experience is the manipulative mother who knows just how to play on her child's feelings.

THE MOON IN CANCER

Sensitive and moody, you have deep security needs that motivate your behavior. This is a dependent and vulnerable Moon. Your instinct is to mother and nurture, but you may smother those around you. You find it hard to let go of the past, clinging possessively. Your insecurity stems from unmet needs and unfulfilled emotions from childhood.

LUNAR FOOD You deeply crave emotional sustenance and validation of your powerful feelings. You need a secure home base.

MOTHER You seek nurturing, comfort, and emotional closeness: overwhelming mother love. You may experience being smothered by a possessive mother who holds you too close.

The sensitive romantic Moon in Cancer is a sucker for the "hearts and flowers" routine.

☽ | The Moon in Leo, Virgo, Libra, Scorpio

THE MOON IN LEO

This is a generous, warm, heart-centered Moon with overwhelming pride. The emotions are fiery and the instinctual needs are strong. Perhaps the most powerful need is that of being made to feel special. You want to be looked up to, worshiped, and adored. To achieve this you are not above playing emotional games and indulging in manipulative ploys. If you are ignored or slighted, then you retreat into standoffishness and wounded dignity. The Leo Moon is the drama queen of the zodiac!

LUNAR FOOD You crave adulation and power.

MOTHER You seek a warm, affectionate mother who is a playmate and an entertainer. What you may experience is the "queen bee." Everything has to revolve her and she demands constant attention from her offspring.

THE MOON IN VIRGO

This is a picky, prudish Moon. Your urge is toward purity and cleanliness, and you may be overly fussy in trying to control life so that the forces of the unconscious do not rise up and overwhelm you. You fear being emotionally engulfed and have a tendency to rationalize your feelings. With your urge toward altruism and service, you care deeply for the needs of others and may be willing to sacrifice yourself to their needs.

LUNAR FOOD You crave reward and recognition for services rendered but are too modest to seek this out.

MOTHER You seek a mother who is perfect. What you may experience is the cold, critical mother who sets impossibly high standards.

THE MOON IN LIBRA

Your strongest urge is toward relationship. Your tendency is to lose yourself in the needs of another. Romantic and glamorous, you adapt and compromise in order to please. You create a malignant "niceness" as you submerge your true

The Moon in Virgo is seeking purity and the perfection of motherhood: the Virgin Mary.

feelings in the needy desire to find wholeness in another. Everything has to feel "right" – you crave harmony and will do everything possible to maintain this. This may sound selfless, but there can be an inherent selfishness at the heart of the Libra Moon.

LUNAR FOOD You crave admiration and companionship and are nourished by peace and beauty.

MOTHER You desire a "nice" mother who will create a beautiful peaceful environment. What you may experience is a mother who is pleasant on the surface but inherently selfish and demands that her need for relationship is met by her child.

THE MOON IN SCORPIO

The most instinctual, overwhelming Moon; traumatic emotions run deep. Needs are intense and compulsive, erupting forcefully from the unconscious. Yours is a jealous nature. Power struggles are a fact of life. This cathartic Moon makes many trips into taboo areas of life. You have to face your own darkness to find insights and healing that transform this alienated Moon.

LUNAR FOOD You crave intensity and all-consuming passion. Emotionally nourished, are empowered. Deprived, you retreat into abusive power.

MOTHER You seek an emotionally intense mother who provides insightful nurturing leading to personal empowerment. What you often experience is the wrathful, devouring mother who lives her own unlived life through the total control of her offspring.

☾ | The Moon in Sagittarius, Capricorn, Aquarius, Pisces

THE MOON IN SAGITTARIUS

You impulsively act out your fiery emotions and then regret it. Your warm heart conflicts with your instinctual needs. Strongly driven by an urge for emotional freedom, you fear commitment. You dislike emotional neediness or coercion and can be insensitive to other people's feelings.

LUNAR FOOD You crave flattery and attention yourself, and can live off discussing other people's feelings.

MOTHER You seek a companionable mother. The archetypal Sagittarian Mother is freedom-loving and spontaneous, but may be haphazard and unable to provide the discipline you need.

THE MOON IN CAPRICORN

Capricorn Moon finds it easier to express affection with gifts than with words.

You find it difficult to show your feelings. With a deep lack of confidence and a strong sense of responsibility, you carry the world on your shoulders. Your driving urge is toward doing what is right. This is the Moon of "oughts" and "shoulds." Childhood may have been emotionally stultifying. You were approved of when you conformed and set great store by "success." Failure is an emotional disaster for you.

LUNAR FOOD You crave approval and desire emotional control.

MOTHER You desire a mother who provides consistent discipline with boundaries that allow space to develop autonomy. What you often experience is a cold, controlling mother who demands conformity

The Moon in Aquarius often feels cut off from the emotional life shared by the rest of humanity, while Moon in Pisces prefers fantasy...

THE MOON IN AQUARIUS

Emotionally independent, you need space and yet can feel isolated from the rest of humanity. Emotional pressure makes you retreat. You prefer to study emotions rather than experience them. "Bad" emotions are not acceptable to you. Nevertheless, you have deep instinctual needs that motivate your life. You have a drive toward revolutionizing the social order and want to better the lot of humanity, for which you care deeply.

LUNAR FOOD You find your emotional nourishment in social contacts but you long for emotional intimacy with that special person who appreciates your need for space.

MOTHER You need a mother who gives you freedom combined with discipline. What you often experience is an unstable mother, an unconventional mother who embarrasses you.

THE MOON IN PISCES

This is a highly sensitive, escapist Moon. Real life is a little too harsh for you, so you seek solace in fantasy. You long for the self-immolation of blissful union. Searching for the perfect relationship, you settle for less in your desire to be one and rarely separate emotionally from past lovers. By far the most emotional of the Moons, you sway this way and that as each passing emotion overwhelms you. Lacking boundaries, you are acutely aware of the pain of other people.

LUNAR FOOD Other people are the food craved by this symbiotic Moon. You desire an emotionally melding relationship above all else.

MOTHER You seek a sensitive, sympathetic mother. What you may often experience is a mother who engulfs you, leaving you no room for individuality.

☿ | Mercury

Mercury shows how you express yourself and how you think. This is a mental, inquisitive planet, encompassing intellect and reason, mind and thought, deduction and curiosity. It has the ability to bring together disparate pieces of information and synthesize them. How these abilities flow is determined by the sign and house in which Mercury is placed.

How you think

The way that you think is governed by the placement of Mercury. In an earth sign, Mercury indicates a practical and orderly thinker who deals with one thing at a time. In a water sign, it shows an imaginative dreamer who may have trouble bringing ideas into practical reality. In the fire signs, Mercury is fast and innovative but practicality is not a strong point. In the air signs, there is a quickness of mind that is inventive and versatile, but you have a tendency to live in your head.

Finding Mercury

Mercury is often in the same sign as your Sun and rarely strays more than a sign away. If you read the interpretation for Mercury in your Sun-sign and those on either side, you will recognize where your Mercury falls.

MERCURY THROUGH THE SIGNS

Mercury in Aries asks: "How can I best express myself?" Quick-thinking, confident, self-willed, and argumentative, you have no trouble at all when communicating your ideas, but find it difficult to listen.

Mercury in Taurus asks: "What is the best way I can plan to meet my need for security?" Slow and methodical, your thoughts are directed toward practical matters with little time for idle speculation.

Mercury is the closest planet to the Sun and acts as a messenger between the self and the rest of the personality – or the outside world.

LE PENS

Mercury in Gemini asks: "How can I communicate my ideas?" Logical, inquisitive, and versatile, you are one of the great communicators because of the fluent way you express your eclectic knowledge.

Mercury in Cancer asks: "What is the best way for me to express my feelings?" Your retentive mind is dominated by your emotions and your thought processes are subjective.

Mercury in Leo asks: "How can I meet my need to be special?" You form your opinions quickly and hold on to them firmly, especially when confronted with another point of view.

Mercury in Virgo asks: "How can I perfect my intellectual skills?" Analytical, discriminating, and overly critical, you want to use your mind to organize and improve your world.

Mercury in Libra asks: "How can I please everyone?" Your vacillating mind is surprisingly sharp when planning strategies and finding ways to reconcile opposing points of view.

Mercury in Scorpio asks: "How might I use my mind to master the world?" Incisive, penetrating, and manipulative, your mind is governed by strong instinctual beliefs. You are attracted to all things mysterious and hidden.

Mercury in Sagittarius asks: "What does it all mean?" This restless, wide-ranging, and philosophical mind is concerned with fundamental truths and enjoys exploring many different belief systems.

Mercury in Capricorn asks: "What is the best way for me to succeed?" This carefully controlled mind is capable of constructive and practical thought.

Mercury in Aquarius asks: "How can I improve the lot of my fellow humans?" Inventive and socially aware, yours is an eccentric and free-thinking mind.

Mercury in Pisces asks: "How can I express my vision out to the world?" Imaginative and intuitive, you can, however, be subject to gullibility and confusion.

This talkative planet cannot be without a means of communication – the mobile phone was invented for Mercury-ruled Gemini.

"The Thinker" sums up the qualities of intellectual Mercury.

♀ | Venus

Voluptuous and romantic, Venus is the planet of relationships. She indicates how easily your needs for emotional satisfaction are met and where you seek your satisfaction. She is attraction in action and shows you your values and your feminine nature. Venus also indicates how you feel about yourself and what you believe you deserve from love.

The planet of love

In a man's chart, Venus shows the type of woman you will be attracted to. In a woman's chart, it represents the way you will present your femininity to the world. In both sexes, Venus is eroticism as well as romantic love.

Finding Venus

Venus is rarely more than one sign away from your Sun (although if your Sun is at the beginning or end of a sign, Venus may be two signs away). Check out all the possible placements.

The planet Venus is deeply veiled in swirling clouds. Like her astrological counterpart, it is difficult to perceive the nature of Venus with a casual glance.

VENUS THROUGH THE SIGNS

Venus in Aries has a siren call. Hedonistic and demanding, you have strong sexual needs. Men with this placement are attracted to dominant women.

Venus in Taurus represents sensuality personified. Reliable and faithful, you will find deep satisfaction in marriage. Men with this type of placement find themselves profoundly attracted to voluptuous women.

Venus in Gemini is born to excel at the subtle art of flirtation. Charming, fickle, and emotionally detached, however, you dislike commitment. Men with this placement seek an intellectual companion.

Venus in Cancer is the eternal homemaker. You are sympathetic and caring but you can be emotionally possessive. Men with Venus in Cancer seek a maternal partner, someone to mother them.

Venus in Leo is amorous and erotic. Constantly seeking admiration, you love the whirl and glamor of the social scene. Men with this placement will seek a strong woman, or perhaps a trophy wife.

Voluptuous Venus is the embodiment of every man's desire. Made for love, she may have some darkly erotic surprises in store.

Venus in Virgo is shy and retiring, but beneath the demure exterior a sexual siren may lurk. Men with this placement seek the perfect woman.

Venus in Libra is made for love. Romantic and accommodating, you are happy to be a "significant other." Men with this placement seek a charming companion to delight the eye.

Venus in Scorpio may have the Scorpion's sting. Passionate and jealous, this is a darkly erotic lover. Men with this placement seek a dark temptress – you like to gamble with danger.

Venus in Sagittarius is generous and warm-hearted, but can be promiscuous. You value freedom above the security of marriage. Men with this placement are attracted to women who seem to promise the world but may fail to deliver.

Venus in Capricorn is cool on the surface and a sexual furnace within. You need a stable relationship so that you will feel safe. Only then will you be ready to discard your inhibitions. Men with this placement seek a self-contained woman who is always in control, or a status symbol wife or mistress.

Venus in Aquarius is unconventional, detached, and somewhat quirky. You prefer friendship to emotional ties. Men with Venus in Aquarius seek an intellectual companion who challenges the norm.

Venus in Pisces is seduction personified. Easily influenced by your feelings, you move fluidly from one relationship to another always in search of eternal romance. Men with this placement seek the embodiment of their fantasy.

♂ | Mars

Virile Mars is lust, libido, will, and the aggressive urge. Action personified, this planet is concerned with self-preservation. Mars shows how you meet your challenges and how you assert yourself. The position of Mars in your chart indicates how you deal with your sexual energy. In a woman's chart, it describes the kind of man to whom you are attracted.

Bold, virile, and assertive, Mars epitomizes desire and sexual libido.

The virile warrior

Mars shows how your passion flows and how easily you assert yourself. Mythical Mars was a bold warrior. The position of Mars describes how the aggressive urge is expressed. In fire signs, Mars is passionate and self-assertive; in earth signs Mars is restrained and sensual. In water signs, Mars is unlikely to be immediately apparent; in air signs, the aggression and passion is channeled into ideas.

Finding Mars

You need a birthchart to ascertain the position of Mars.

MARS THROUGH THE SIGNS

Mars in Aries is lusty, aggressive, and impatient. Courageous and strong-willed, you go all out for what you want. Women with this placement seek a self-confident, virile, macho man.

Mars in Taurus is determined, sensual, and immovable. Self-assertion is restrained but anger explodes. Women with this placement seek a stable lover who is very affectionate.

Mars in Gemini is charming but fickle. The need for self-expression is urgent but passion goes into words, not actions. Women with this Mars prefer smooth talkers.

Mars in Cancer is not likely to be self-assertive in a direct way. Although strong-willed, this is hidden behind a passivity beneath which passion flows. Women with this placement seek a strong, protective man.

Mars in Leo wants to be top of the heap. Self-expression is dramatic and assertive. This is a creative placement. Women with Mars in Leo seek a man that they can look up to and admire.

Mars in Virgo is repressive and restrained. Passion is earthy, but controlled. Self-assertion is tempered with caution. Virgo–Mars women tend to be drawn to a consistent, practical man.

Mars in Libra is laid-back and avoids arguments. Energy is channeled into mutual harmony rather than self-assertion. Women with this placement seek a charming man to lead them into marriage.

Mars in Scorpio is intense and deeply passionate. This rarely shows on the surface, but you always get what you want. Women with this placement are attracted to sexy, powerful men.

Mars in Sagittarius is an enthusiastic traveler. Enormous energy is put into exploring life. Spontaneous passion can also run high. Women with this placement seek a free-spirited companion.

Mars in Capricorn is strongly determined with a powerful sex drive. Self-assertion is directed toward success. Women with this placement seek a highly successful man.

Mars in Aquarius is strong-willed with radical ideas. You may channel your passion into ideals. Women with this placement seek a fighter with strong principles.

Mars in Pisces may have a strong sex drive but is easily sidetracked. Women with this placement look for a fairy-tale lover.

A woman with Mars in Pisces will seek a fairy-tale, Prince Charming lover.

Clint Eastwood as a typical martian hero: the Macho Man. Eastwood's Mars in Aries positively smoulders, making him irresistible to women and yet admired by men.

♃ | Jupiter

Jupiter is the planet of expansion and good fortune. This is the urge to grow and to find your purpose. Jupiter gives you something to believe in. Associated with "lady luck," this is the gambler's planet. Under the influence of Jupiter you are not afraid to take a risk, though you may regret it later.

Growth

Jupiter shows the way in which you expand and grow. It is your core belief system, your faith, and your optimism. It is also where you are prone to excess.

The cycle of opportunity

Jupiter takes 12 years to travel around the zodiac. When Jupiter reaches its place in your birthchart (at age 12, 24, 36, etc.), a new cycle of opportunity opens up.

At the start of the Jupiter cycle you may have an idea, take up a new opportunity, or start a new job. For the first three years you work hard, and at the end of that time you will know whether you are going to be successful or not. If you are, then at six years you will begin to reap the rewards. At nine years, the cycle starts to close down to make way for something new – then the whole cycle starts up again. By attuning to this cycle, you can time your projects for maximum growth.

With Jupiter urging you on, taking a risk is not a problem!

Finding Jupiter

You need a birthchart to ascertain Jupiter's position.

JUPITER THROUGH THE SIGNS

Jupiter in Aries is headstrong and "Me" oriented. It is prone to exaggeration and going "over the top."

Jupiter in Taurus is ambitious and adores luxury. There may be a tendency to put on weight.

Jupiter in Gemini is exceedingly talkative, prone to telling tall tales, and will take risks. There is an urge to distribute information.

Jupiter in Cancer is strongly protective and dedicated to caring for others.

Jupiter in Leo makes a big impression. This is a high-minded placement.

Jupiter in Virgo is unassuming and gently ambitious. Expansion is through mental productivity.

Jupiter in Libra seeks luxury and companionship. Hedonism may run rife.

Jupiter in Scorpio pushes back taboos and is not afraid to explore the forbidden frontiers of hidden knowledge.

Jupiter in Sagittarius exaggerates wildly, is willing to take a gamble on life, and enjoys it to the full.

Jupiter in Capricorn may be far-sighted and wise, or, on the contrary, may feel constricted within rigid boundaries.

Jupiter in Aquarius is prone to whims of eccentricity but humanitarian ideals are emphasized.

Jupiter in Pisces is religiously inclined but may retreat into escapist fantasy. The way forward is through imagination and the arts.

♄ | Saturn

Saturn is hard, cold, and bleak. This is the planet of discipline and boundaries. It is where you strive to hold on to what you have achieved, to keep order in your life. Without Saturn, things would run riot, but the planet may be overly controlling. Saturn is concerned with form, structure, and time. It indicates the blocks you meet in life. Saturn is also karma.

The shower of the way

Saturn points you along the path of duty and destiny. This planet delineates the boundaries of your known world, but it is also the place where you must push through those boundaries in order to grow. Blockages you encounter under Saturn make you stronger.

The life review

Saturn returns to its natal place once every 28–9 years. This means that at the ages of 28–9 and 57 you will undergo a life review. If you are following your true path and fulfilling your purpose, then your life expands. If you are not, you meet a life crisis in which you must reassess your goals. Saturn is a hard taskmaster, but holds much wisdom.

Finding Saturn

You need a birthchart to identify the sign in which your Saturn is placed.

SATURN THROUGH THE SIGNS

Saturn in Aries checks natural impulsiveness. You often feel frustrated, although Saturn can give you the discipline to go forward.

Saturn in Taurus has dogged determination and tenacity. Caution is strong and the feelings are controlled.

Saturn in Gemini may be unusually slow of speech and finds communication difficult. There is great seriousness of thought.

Saturn in Cancer is particularly security conscious. You may be inclined to set rigid boundaries to protect those you love.

The rings of Saturn symbolize the strong boundaries of this highly disciplined planet.

Saturn in Leo limits creative power or channels it into rigid outlets. Life may
be difficult and enjoyment blocked.

Saturn in Virgo is extremely conscientious and is not afraid to work very
hard. Detail is overly important.

Saturn in Libra has seemingly endless patience. This placement, however,
may indicate loneliness and difficulty relating to others.

Saturn in Scorpio is reserved and secretive. The emotions may be strongly
controlled or blocked.

Saturn in Sagittarius may undergo a long period of study. A rigid system of
beliefs may be indicated.

Saturn in Capricorn is cautious and careful. This placement has the ability to
work long and hard for carefully planned success.

Saturn in Aquarius may indicate the solitary path of a lone ideologist, but
rational thought is well directed.

Saturn in Pisces is not happy! Planet and sign are diametrically opposed.
Restrictions cause great frustration.

⚷ | Chiron

Chiron wandered into our solar system and its eccentric orbit bridges the planets, creating the possibility of integration and fusion.

The path to evolution, the recently discovered "planet" Chiron indicates where you are wounded, and where you must give up your suffering. This planet is a maverick, with the courage to be different and to stand alone. It unites paradoxes and dilemmas, integrates opposites, and heals your pain. Chiron is a key.

The wounded healer

In myth, Chiron was both warrior and healer. He was wounded by one of the heroes he tutored, but because he was immortal he could not die. He could not heal either, so he had to live with his wound. Eventually Chiron found the way to heal himself through the renunciation of his immortality.

Chiron is a bridging planet. It moves from an orbit between Saturn and Uranus to one between Saturn and Jupiter. It brings the impersonal energies of the outer planets into personal consciousness. It is the key to moving beyond the purely personal and encompassing the whole. It shows you what you must eliminate from your life in order to free yourself from suffering and heal your karmic wounds.

Finding Chiron

Chiron has a most eccentric orbit, spending a short time in some signs and a longer time in others. Chiron returns to its natal position at age 51, bringing an opportunity to heal the wound.

CHIRON THROUGH THE SIGNS

Chiron in Aries is the key to the self. The wound is in the ego. Healing comes through becoming centered within your true self.

Chiron in Taurus is the key to personal resources. The wound is fear of loss of security. Healing comes through developing inner security.

Chiron in Gemini is the key to communication blockages. The wound stems from difficulty in making yourself heard. Healing comes in speaking out.

Chiron in Cancer is the key to maternal and emotional wounds. Healing

In mythology, Chiron was king of the centaurs. He had the gifts of healing and spiritual warriorship.

comes through emotional detachment and an inner feeling of safety.

Chiron in Leo is the key to unblocking creativity. The wound is rooted in self-expression. Healing comes in finding your own inner uniqueness.

Chiron in Virgo is the key to service. The wound is in being taken for granted. Healing comes through unconditional love.

Chiron in Libra is the key to healing wounded relationships. Healing comes when you find yourself whole.

Chiron in Scorpio is the key to power. The wound is in the abuse and misuse of power. Healing comes through mastery of personal empowerment.

Chiron in Sagittarius is the key to philosophy. The wound is in the belief system. Healing comes in finding a personal philosophy to live by.

Chiron in Capricorn is the key to success. The wound is failure in the material world. Healing comes about through recognition of your strengths.

Chiron in Aquarius is the key to humanity. The wound is separation from the collective. Healing comes through the reconciliation of the needs of the individual with society.

Chiron in Pisces is the key to healing separation. The wound is living in a fantasy of self-obliteration. Healing comes about through union with the divine.

In Leo, Chiron can be the key to healing wounded creativity.

⛢ | Uranus

This is the planet of original thought. Unpredictable and catalytic, the effect of Uranus is sudden and unexpected, like being struck by lightning. Uranus is change – the intuitive flash that alters your life. You have to let go of everything that you have outgrown and that is now worn out. Rebellious and nonconformist, Uranus shows you where you struggle to be free of past restrictions and where opportunity can strike out of the blue.

Uranus has a strange and eccentric orbit, spending many years in one sign and few in another.

Crisis and opportunity

Uranus is the rebel planet, not given to conformity. It is associated with crisis and opportunity. It rattles people's cages, setting them free through unusual and unexpected events. Not everyone appreciates the suddenness of Uranian change. There are times when you need to rescue the baby who has inadvertently been disposed of with the bathwater. Uranus cannot distinguish between what is good from the past and what has to go.

The midlife crisis

During the average lifetime of 84 years, Uranus makes one circuit of the zodiac. You particularly notice its effect somewhere between 40–44 years of age. This is known as the midlife crisis – the time when disruption, dissatisfaction, and unavoidable change signal that your life must be transformed.

Finding Uranus

Impossible. You need a birthchart.

The discovery of Uranus coincided with the start of the Industrial Revolution.

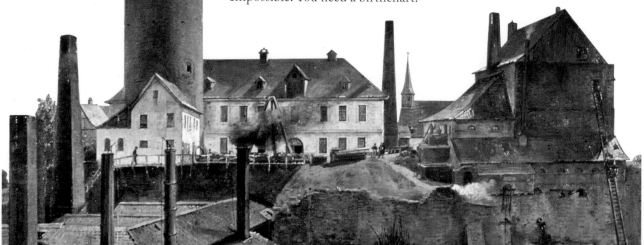

Uranus is intuitive, rebellious, and brilliant, the planet for sudden changes of direction.

URANUS THROUGH THE SIGNS

Uranus in Aries is a loose cannon. It is highly unpredictable and extremely self-willed, a placement that is disruptive and independent.

Uranus in Taurus exerts unbearable tension. This is the immovable object meeting irresistible force. Something has to blow.

Uranus in Gemini is verbally unpredictable and exceedingly intuitive, with highly inventive and original thought processes.

Uranus in Cancer can be emotionally unstable but may need to break out of always taking care of others.

Uranus in Leo can be exceedingly arrogant. However, there is also a quality of charismatic leadership.

Uranus in Virgo can lead you to follow the latest health fads and promotes an interest in unconventional healing.

Uranus in Libra produces some explosive relationships. You may need to break out and be yourself.

Uranus in Scorpio Ouch! This combination can be cruel and emotionally unpredictable. It seeks a new understanding of life and death.

Uranus in Sagittarius is exceedingly freedom-loving and may become the rebel or revolutionary. Unconventional beliefs direct life.

Uranus in Capricorn may indicate brilliance, especially in the business world, but this placement can be eccentric and highly-strung.

Uranus in Aquarius forces through changes that benefit humanity. If all else has failed, you may resort to terrorism.

Uranus in Pisces results in a powerful intuition but may be at the mercy of ever-changing emotions.

The Uranian mid-life crisis is rather like being struck by lightning.

Ψ | Neptune

*The slippery planet of greatest
extremes, Neptune moves from the
depths of illusion, delusion, confusion,
and deception through imagination
and fantasy to artistic inspiration and
the highest states of mystical consciousness.
This planet makes it hard to distinguish
between fantasy and reality, and questions exactly
what is real. Used constructively, Neptune brings
enlightenment. Used destructively, everything disintegrates.*

*Escaping into the fantasy
world of virtual reality
has more than a touch of
Neptune about it. Which is
illusion and what is real?*

*Neptune shows you what you aspire to at your highest
level and where the delusive traps surround you.*

The great escape

Neptune inhabits a world that is diffuse and hypnotic.
Under the influence of this imprecise planet you want to
escape, to slip away. That slipping away may mean into
inspiration and ecstasy, but it might just as easily be into
drugs or alcohol. Only Neptune knows which is which.
Lacking boundaries, Neptune has problems living in
the everyday world. Perceiving the world through nebulous
Neptune is like peering through a fog. Everything is
blurred and unreal. Yet, if Neptune
inhabits a sign where its energy can be
harnessed, you become the inspired poet,
the singer of songs. If it does not, you may
sacrifice yourself to the collective need. Neptune is the natural
martyr and knows exactly where your guilt button is located.

A beautiful blue-green planet, Neptune symbolizes the highest artistic inspiration and spiritual endeavor – and the greatest illusions!

Finding Neptune

Neptune moves comparatively slowly through the signs. In 1916 it moved out of Cancer and will not return there for 165 years. The table shown alongside gives Neptune's possible placements:

1916–1928	Leo
1928–1943	Virgo
1943–1956	Libra
1956–1970	Scorpio
1970–1984	Sagittarius
1984–1998	Capricorn
1998–2011	Aquarius
2011–2025	Pisces

NEPTUNE THROUGH THE SIGNS

Neptune in Leo aspires to great creative works, but the ideas may be too vague or too grandiose to put into practice.

Neptune in Virgo aspires to service and self-sacrifice for the good of others. The delusion may come in the confusion between servitude and true service.

Neptune in Libra aspires to romantic love. The confusion lies in thinking that charm is all that it takes.

Neptune in Scorpio aspires to sublimate personal power to spiritual ideals. The delusion lies in attributing all your yearnings to a higher power.

Neptune in Sagittarius aspires to spiritual practice. The delusion lies in false gurus and inappropriate gods.

Neptune in Capricorn aspires to the brotherhood of humanity expressed through religion. The delusion lies in worshiping the false god of materialism.

Neptune in Aquarius aspires to humanism and humanitarianism. The danger lies in confusing ideology with rationality.

Neptune in Pisces aspires to a total merging. The delusion lies in the confusion of not being able to distinguish between escapism and spiritual inspiration.

Neptune's influence can be seen most clearly in those who enjoy a rich life of the imagination, like the poet Seamus Heaney.

♇ | Pluto

Sheathed in ice and way out of reach of all but the most powerful telescopes, Pluto's small size belies its powerful influence on our lives.

Pluto is concerned with power and transmutation. It is a dark and devious planet of compulsions, obsessions, abuses, and misuses. It is all that is taboo. It is also the planet of purification and regeneration; the treasure that lies at the heart of darkness. The placement of Pluto shows how easily we can regenerate ourselves.

Regeneration

Pluto is the urge to regenerate, to be born anew. Pluto is also concerned with elimination, especially of things that pollute the psyche. It shows the toxicity of the past and what must be released so that something new can flower. It is the urge to transmute and refine your innermost self. Nevertheless, Pluto is most powerful at the collective level.

Used wisely, Pluto transmutes the darkest of experiences; used unwisely, Pluto is self-destructive and resentful. This is the planet of power, abuse and misuse of power; and of manipulation. It is also the planet of empowerment and magical transformation.

Finding Pluto

Pluto moves very slowly and can take several generations to pass through a sign. The table alongside will give you your Pluto position:

♇	
1914–1939	Cancer
1939–1957	Leo
1957–1972	Virgo
1972–1984	Libra
1984–1995	Scorpio
1995–2008	Sagittarius
2008–2022	Capricorn

PLUTO THROUGH THE SIGNS

Pluto in Cancer urges the collective into social change. While it is sentimentally attached to the family and idealizes it, the passage of Pluto through Cancer witnessed the beginning of the disintegration of family life – although with this as your placement, you try to hold on at all cost.

Pluto in Leo signaled the rise of the "Me" generation. The individual was separated from the collective, aided and abetted by Pluto's transforming power. Born with this placement, you direct and star in your own movie.

Pluto in Virgo brings you face-to-face with entrenched values. The nuclear family breaks up, employment is no longer for life, and health issues come to

When Pluto passed through Cancer the world was urged into social change. The rise of Russian communism, spearheaded by Lenin, brought plutonian abuse of power alongside a brave new world.

the fore. With this placement, you are faced with the purification of planet earth.

Pluto in Libra challenged the assumptions relationships were based on. If you were born with this placement, you have to eliminate old, inappropriate ways of relating and revolutionize your relationships on all levels.

Pluto in Scorpio dredges up all that is polluted and worn out. It challenges existing taboos and reveals what is hidden and repressed. Regeneration for this placement comes about through working along with Pluto in order to bring things into the light.

Pluto in Sagittarius has the challenge of confronting old, no longer workable ideologies and finding a new way forward. It pinpoints where these outgrown patterns of being must be transmuted.

Pluto in Capricorn is the start of a new evolutionary journey. Conflict between worn out conservatism and the implementation of new social policies needs to be worked through resulting in the creation of a healthy interdependence.

Pluto challenges us to confront all that is taboo. We rarely see Pluto creeping up to snatch us into his underworld, but we feel the effect.

The Angles

The angles are orientation points. The Ascendant is the sign rising over the horizon at birth. Its opposite point is the Descendant. The Midheaven is the highest point that the Sun appears to traverse on its path around the chart, and its opposite point is the IC (imum coeli). The Ascendant is the face that we present to the world, the Descendant where we go out to meet others, the Midheaven what we strive for, and the IC our deepest roots.

RELATING TO THE WORLD

How you relate to the inner and outer worlds is shown by the angles. These are orientation points that help you to find your way around a birthchart. The sign on the angles affects how you interact with the world. A powerful Ascendant sign, for example, can overcome the shyness of a retiring Sun-sign, presenting a confident face to cover a lack of confidence. The Midheaven placed in an enterprising sign strengthens ambition in a passive Sun-sign. (You need a birthchart to identify your Midheaven and IC.)

THE ASCENDANT

The Ascendant is also known as the rising sign because it is the sign coming up over the horizon at the moment of your birth. This is your public face and it will always be the first impression that people receive of you. The Ascendant describes how you adapt to, and the impact you will have on, your environment. It may well also be a mask that you use to conceal your true nature.

The Ascendant also shows how you adapt to physical incarnation and how well coordinated your body will be. With an earth-sign Ascendant, you are at home in your body and move with grace and confidence. With a fire-sign Ascendant, you are in a hurry and do not always cooperate with your body. With an air-sign Ascendant, your movements will be quick and light. With a water-sign Ascendant, your body flows fluidly.

The angles on your chart will always be in the shape of a cross with the Ascendant to the left as you look at it, and the Midheaven toward the top.

Midheaven

Ascendant
Horizon
Descendant

I.C.

Finding Your Ascendant

Finding your Ascendant

• Using the tables that follow, select the nearest latitude to the place where you were born.

• Place a ruler on your time of birth (making allowance for daylight saving, if applicable).

• Line the ruler up with your birthday on the opposite side.

• The ruler will pass through a zodiac sign – your most probable Ascendant. Check the interpretation. If it does not seem to fit, read the signs on either side.

Date		Ascendant	Time
JAN	10 / 20 / 30	♎ / ♏	1 / 2
FEB	10 / 20 / 29		3 / 4
MAR	10 / 20 / 30	♐ / ♑ / ♒ / ♓ / ♈	5 / 6 AM
APR	10 / 20 / 30	♉ / ♊	7 / 8
MAY	10 / 20 / 30	♋	9 / 10
JUN	10 / 20 / 30	♌ / ♍	11 / 12 NOON
JUL	10 / 20 / 30	♎ / ♏	1 / 2
AUG	10 / 20 / 30	♐	3 / 4
SEP	10 / 20 / 30	♑ / ♒ / ♓ / ♈ / ♉	5 / 6 PM
OCT	10 / 20 / 30	♊	7 / 8
NOV	10 / 20 / 30	♋ / ♌	9 / 10
DEC	10 / 20 / 30	♍	11 / 12

LONDON 51° 32'N
CALGARY 51° 32'N
CARDIFF 51° 32'N

Date		Ascendant	Time
JAN	10 / 20 / 30	♎ / ♏	1 / 2
FEB	10 / 20 / 29		3 / 4
MAR	10 / 20 / 30	♐ / ♑ / ♒ / ♓ / ♈	5 / 6 AM
APR	10 / 20 / 30	♉ / ♊	7 / 8
MAY	10 / 20 / 30	♋	9 / 10
JUN	10 / 20 / 30	♌ / ♍	11 / 12 NOON
JUL	10 / 20 / 30	♎ / ♏	1 / 2
AUG	10 / 20 / 30	♐	3 / 4
SEP	10 / 20 / 30	♑ / ♒ / ♓ / ♈ / ♉	5 / 6 PM
OCT	10 / 20 / 30	♊	7 / 8
NOV	10 / 20 / 30	♋ / ♌	9 / 10
DEC	10 / 20 / 30	♍	11 / 12

TOKYO 35° 41'N
LOS ANGELES 34° 00'N
MEMPHIS, TENN. 35° 07'N

Date		Ascendant	Time
JAN	10 / 20 / 30	♎ / ♏	1 / 2
FEB	10 / 20 / 29		3 / 4
MAR	10 / 20 / 30	♐ / ♑ / ♒ / ♓ / ♈	5 / 6 AM
APR	10 / 20 / 30	♉ / ♊	7 / 8
MAY	10 / 20 / 30	♋	9 / 10
JUN	10 / 20 / 30	♌ / ♍	11 / 12 NOON
JUL	10 / 20 / 30	♎ / ♏	1 / 2
AUG	10 / 20 / 30	♐	3 / 4
SEP	10 / 20 / 30	♑ / ♒ / ♓ / ♈ / ♉	5 / 6 PM
OCT	10 / 20 / 30	♊	7 / 8
NOV	10 / 20 / 30	♋ / ♌	9 / 10
DEC	10 / 20 / 30	♍	11 / 12

NEW ORLEANS 29° 57'N
HOUSTON, TEXAS 29° 45'N
JACKSONVILLE 30° 15'N

Date	Ascendant	Time
JAN 10	♎	1
JAN 20		2
JAN 30	♏	3
FEB 10		
FEB 20	♐	4
FEB 29		5
MAR 10	♑	
MAR 20	♒ ♓	6 AM
MAR 30	♈	7
APR 10	♉	
APR 20	♊	8
APR 30		9
MAY 10	♋	
MAY 20		10
MAY 30	♌	
JUN 10		11
JUN 20	♍	12 NOON
JUN 30		
JUL 10	♎	1
JUL 20		2
JUL 30	♏	
AUG 10		3
AUG 20	♐	4
AUG 30		
SEP 10	♑ ♒	5
SEP 20	♓ ♈	
SEP 30	♉	6 PM
OCT 10	♊	7
OCT 20		8
OCT 30		
NOV 10	♋	9
NOV 20	♌	10
NOV 30		
DEC 10		11
DEC 20	♍	12
DEC 30		

TORONTO 43° 40'N
MILWAUKEE 43° 09'N

Date	Ascendant	Time
JAN 10	♎	1
JAN 20		2
JAN 30	♏	3
FEB 10		
FEB 20	♐	4
FEB 29		5
MAR 10	♑	
MAR 20	♒ ♓	6 AM
MAR 30	♈	7
APR 10	♉	
APR 20	♊	8
APR 30		9
MAY 10		
MAY 20	♋	10
MAY 30	♌	
JUN 10		11
JUN 20	♍	12 NOON
JUN 30		
JUL 10	♎	1
JUL 20		2
JUL 30	♏	
AUG 10		3
AUG 20	♐	4
AUG 30		
SEP 10	♑ ♒	5
SEP 20	♓ ♈	
SEP 30	♉	6 PM
OCT 10	♊	7
OCT 20		8
OCT 30		
NOV 10	♋	9
NOV 20	♌	10
NOV 30		
DEC 10		11
DEC 20	♍	12
DEC 30		

SAN FRANCISCO 37° 47'N
WASHINGTON DC 37° 47'N

Date	Ascendant	Time
JAN 10	♎	1
JAN 20		2
JAN 30	♏	3
FEB 10		
FEB 20		4
FEB 29	♐	5
MAR 10	♑	
MAR 20	♒ ♓	6 AM
MAR 30	♈	7
APR 10	♉	
APR 20	♊	8
APR 30		9
MAY 10		
MAY 20	♋	10
MAY 30		
JUN 10	♌	11
JUN 20	♍	12 NOON
JUN 30		
JUL 10		1
JUL 20	♎	2
JUL 30		3
AUG 10	♏	
AUG 20	♐	4
AUG 30		5
SEP 10	♑ ♒	
SEP 20	♓ ♈	6 PM
SEP 30	♉	7
OCT 10	♊	
OCT 20		8
OCT 30		9
NOV 10	♋	
NOV 20	♌	10
NOV 30		
DEC 10		11
DEC 20	♍	12
DEC 30		

ROME 41° 54'N
BOSTON 42° 18'N
CHICAGO 41° 50'N
DETROIT 42° 22'N

Date	Ascendant	Time
JAN 10	♎	1
JAN 20		2
JAN 30	♏	3
FEB 10		
FEB 20	♐	4
FEB 29		5
MAR 10	♑	
MAR 20	♒ ♓	6 AM
MAR 30	♈	7
APR 10	♉	
APR 20	♊	8
APR 30		9
MAY 10		
MAY 20		10
MAY 30	♋	
JUN 10		11
JUN 20	♍	12 NOON
JUN 30		
JUL 10	♎	1
JUL 20		2
JUL 30		
AUG 10	♏	3
AUG 20	♐	4
AUG 30		
SEP 10	♑ ♒	5
SEP 20	♓ ♈	
SEP 30	♉	6 PM
OCT 10	♊	7
OCT 20		8
OCT 30		
NOV 10	♋	9
NOV 20	♌	10
NOV 30		
DEC 10		11
DEC 20	♍	12
DEC 30		

NEW YORK 40° 45'N
DENVER 39° 50'N
PITTSBURGH 40° 30'N
SALT LAKE CITY 40° 45'N

Date	Ascendant	Time
JAN 10	♎	1
JAN 20		2
JAN 30	♏	3
FEB 10		
FEB 20	♐	4
FEB 29		5
MAR 10	♑	
MAR 20	♒ ♓	6 AM
MAR 30	♈ ♉	7
APR 10		
APR 20	♊	8
APR 30	♉	9
MAY 10		
MAY 20	♋	10
MAY 30		
JUN 10	♌	11
JUN 20	♍	12 NOON
JUN 30		
JUL 10		1
JUL 20	♎	2
JUL 30	♏	
AUG 10		3
AUG 20	♐	4
AUG 30		
SEP 10	♑ ♒	5
SEP 20	♓ ♈ ♉	
SEP 30		6 PM
OCT 10	♊	7
OCT 20		8
OCT 30		
NOV 10	♋	9
NOV 20	♌	10
NOV 30		
DEC 10		11
DEC 20	♍	12
DEC 30		

EDINBURGH 55° 57'N
GLASGOW 55° 52'N

Date	Ascendant	Time
JAN 10	♎	1
JAN 20		2
JAN 30	♏	3
FEB 10		
FEB 20	♐	4
FEB 29		5
MAR 10	♑	
MAR 20	♒ ♓	6 AM
MAR 30	♈	7
APR 10	♉	
APR 20	♊	8
APR 30		9
MAY 10		
MAY 20		10
MAY 30	♋	
JUN 10		11
JUN 20	♍	12 NOON
JUN 30		
JUL 10		1
JUL 20	♎	2
JUL 30	♏	
AUG 10		3
AUG 20	♐	4
AUG 30		
SEP 10	♑ ♒	5
SEP 20	♓ ♈	
SEP 30	♉	6 PM
OCT 10	♊	7
OCT 20		8
OCT 30		
NOV 10	♋	9
NOV 20	♌	10
NOV 30		
DEC 10		11
DEC 20	♍	12
DEC 30		

PARIS 48° 50'N
SEATTLE 47° 45'N
VANCOUVER 49° 14'N

Astrological Time

An accurate time of birth is essential for a correct natal chart.

Astrologers use Greenwich Mean Time (GMT) in their calculations. If you live in a time zone that is different to GMT, you will need to make the appropriate time adjustment.

TIME ZONES

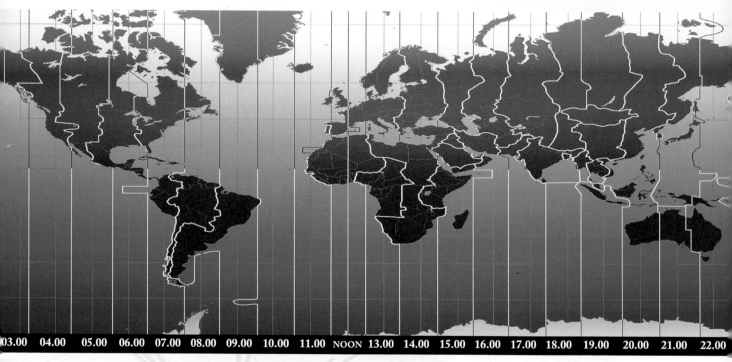

| 03.00 | 04.00 | 05.00 | 06.00 | 07.00 | 08.00 | 09.00 | 10.00 | 11.00 | NOON | 13.00 | 14.00 | 15.00 | 16.00 | 17.00 | 18.00 | 19.00 | 20.00 | 21.00 | 22.00 |

The world is divided into different time zones. Some countries have only one time zone, but bigger countries like the United States need several divisions. If you live east of London, add the time difference to your time of birth. If you live to the west subtract from it your birthtime to give GMT.

BST (UNITED KINGDOM)

Year	Start	End		Year	Start	End		Year	Start	End		Year	Start	End
1920	28 Mar	25 Oct		1940	25 Feb	31 Dec		1954	11 Apr	3 Oct		1974	17 Mar	27 Oct
1921	3 Apr	3 Oct		1941	1 Jan	4 May		1955	17 Apr	2 Oct		1975	16 Mar	26 Oct
1922	26 Mar	8 Apr		1941	10 Aug	31 Dec		1956	22 Apr	7 Oct		1976	21 Mar	24 Oct
1923	22 Mar	16 Sep		1942	1 Jan	5 Apr		1957	14 Apr	6 Oct		1977	20 Mar	23 Oct
1924	13 Mar	21 Sep		1942	9 Aug	31 Dec		1958	20 Apr	5 Oct		1978	19 Mar	29 Oct
1925	19 Mar	4 Oct		1943	1 Jan	4 Apr		1959	19 Apr	4 Oct		1979	18 Mar	28 Oct
1926	18 Mar	3 Oct		1943	15 Aug	31 Dec		1960	10 Apr	2 Oct		1980	16 Mar	26 Oct
1927	10 Mar	2 Oct		1944	1 Jan	2 Apr		1961	26 Apr	29 Oct		1981	29 Mar	25 Oct
1928	22 Mar	7 Oct		1944	17 Sep	31 Dec		1962	25 Mar	28 Oct		1982	28 Mar	24 Oct
1929	21 Mar	6 Oct		1945	1 Jan	2 Apr		1963	31 Mar	27 Oct		1983	27 Mar	23 Oct
1930	13 Mar	5 Oct		1945	15 Jul	7 Oct		1964	22 Mar	25 Oct		1984	25 Mar	28 Oct
1931	19 Mar	4 Oct		1946	14 Apr	6 Oct		1965	21 Mar	24 Oct		1985	31 Mar	27 Oct
1932	17 Mar	2 Oct		1947	16 Mar	13 Apr		1966	20 Mar	23 Oct				
1933	9 Mar	8 Oct		1947	10 Aug	2 Nov		1967	19 Mar	29 Oct		**Double Summer Time**		
1934	22 Mar	7 Oct		1948	14 Mar	31 Oct		1968	18 Feb	31 Dec		1941	4 May	10 Aug
1935	14 Mar	6 Oct		1949	3 Apr	30 Oct		1969	1 Jan	31 Dec		1942	5 Apr	9 Aug
1936	19 Mar	4 Oct		1950	16 Apr	22 Oct		1970	1 Jan	31 Dec		1943	4 Apr	15 Aug
1937	18 Mar	3 Oct		1951	15 Apr	21 Oct		1971	1 Jan	31 Dec		1944	2 Apr	17 Sep
1938	10 Mar	2 Oct		1952	20 Apr	26 Oct		1972	19 Mar	29 Oct		1945	2 Apr	15 Jul
1939	16 Mar	19 Nov		1953	19 Apr	4 Oct		1973	18 Mar	28 Oct		1947	13 Apr	10 Aug

BRITISH SUMMER TIME AND DOUBLE SUMMER TIME

British Summer Time (BST) is an hour ahead of GMT. Deduct one hour from BST to give GMT. Starting in 1986, BST came into operation on the last Sunday in March and ended on the last Sunday in October. Earlier dates are given above. During 1941–7, Double Summer Time was in operation and two hours may have to be deducted from a wartime birth.

DAYLIGHT SAVING TIME (SUMMER TIME) IN THE UNITED STATES

Year	Start	End		Year	Start	End		Year	Start	End		Year	Start	End
1966	24 Apr	30 Oct		1979	29 Apr	28 Oct		1918	31 Mar	27 Oct		1956	29 Apr	30 Sep
1967	30 Apr	29 Oct		1980	27 Apr	26 Oct		1919	30 Mar	26 Oct		1957	27 Apr	29 Sep
1968	28 Apr	27 Oct		1981	26 Apr	25 Oct		1942	9 Feb	31 Dec		1958	27 Apr	28 Sep
1969	27 Apr	26 Oct		1982	25 Apr	31 Oct		1943	1 Jan	31 Dec		1959	26 Apr	27 Sep
1970	26 Apr	25 Oct		1983	24 Apr	30 Oct		1944	1 Jan	31 Dec		1960	24 Apr	25 Sep
1971	25 Apr	24 Oct		1984	29 Apr	28 Oct		1945	1 Jan	30 Sep		1961	30 Apr	24 Sep
1972	30 Apr	29 Oct		1985	28 Apr	27 Oct		1948	14 Mar	1 Jan		1962	29 Sep	28 Oct
1973	29 Apr	27 Oct		1986	27 Apr	26 Oct		1950	30 Apr	24 Sep		1963	28 Apr	27 Oct
1974	28 Apr	27 Oct		1987	26 Apr	25 Oct		1951	29 Apr	30 Sep		1964	26 Apr	25 Oct
1975	27 Apr	26 Oct		1988	24 Apr	30 Oct		1952	27 Apr	28 Sep		1965	25 Apr	31 Oct
1976	25 Apr	31 Oct		1989	30 Apr	29 Oct		1953	26 Apr	27 Sep				
1977	24 Apr	30 Oct		1990	29 Apr	28 Oct		1954	25 Apr	26 Sep				
1978	30 Apr	29 Oct						1955	24 Apr	25 Sep				

AMERICAN DAYLIGHT SAVING

Since 1966, Daylight Saving has been uniform in the US. To calculate GMT, subtract one hour from Daylight Saving Time and adjust according to time differences shown on the Time Zone map.

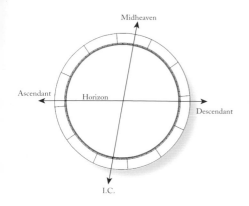

Midheaven

Ascendant

Horizon

Descendant

I.C.

The Cardinal Ascendant

With your Ascendant in a cardinal sign, you appear outgoing and enterprising. This is the quality that gets things moving. The impact you make is immediate. People perceive you as active and confident, full of verve, and ambitious. However, if you have a passive Sun-sign, you may not deliver everything you appear to offer. The impression that an Ascendant makes can be misleading – a deep lethargy can underlie that buzz of activity. But combine a cardinal Ascendant with an outgoing Sun-sign and you have liftoff!

ASCENDANT IN ARIES

You are difficult to ignore! A whirlwind of activity, you burn yourself out quickly unless you learn to pace yourself. People perceive you as assertive, aggressive, and energetic. The problem is, if your Sun-sign is less focused, all that energy goes to waste. You spend time rushing around appearing to be extremely busy, but in reality you are achieving very little.

Your impact on your environment is immediate. Thinking you know best, you do not listen to others. You initiate change and get projects started, then you want to move on. Learning to cooperate and delegate is vital.

ASCENDANT IN CANCER

You appear to be tough and uncompromising, but this exterior covers a soft heart. You consider other people in your drive to get to the top. Ambitious and tenacious, you do not approach things in the same head-on fashion of other cardinal Ascendants. Cancer likes to move in at an angle, sizing things up, then suddenly, before anyone realizes it, you are there.

Your impact on your environment is subtle. You want to make a home for people, to nurture them, and make them comfortable. You prefer to be in positions of authority where you can express this concern.

With the Ascendant in Aries, people see a whirlwind of activity – a real "go-getter."

Even when working in a service industry, there will be a touch of authority about the Capricorn Ascendant.

A Libra Ascendant shows itself in luxurious and ostentatious – but always tasteful – surroundings.

ASCENDANT IN LIBRA

You show a charming face to the world. Likeable and easy to get along with, you have an equable temperament – until you find that things are not going the way you want them to. You have a surprisingly tough side under that pleasant face. You can be selfish, but find a means to compromise rather than initiate head-on confrontation. People may accuse you of manipulation, which hurts your feelings. You are the "people pleaser" *par excellence*.

Always well groomed, your impact on your environment manifests itself in harmonious surroundings. Glamorous and sumptuous, there is a touch of luxury about a Libra Ascendant.

ASCENDANT IN CAPRICORN

You are ambitious and earnest, often looking as though you carry a burden or heavy responsibility. This is not surprising because you take life very seriously and you are absolutely determined to get to the top.

People notice you because of your air of authority and your appearance, which is formal and conservative. You frequently have a touch of gray about your person. Your impact on the environment is strong. You like to organize your own life as well as other people's and can be authoritarian and somewhat judgmental. You want to support and preserve the status quo.

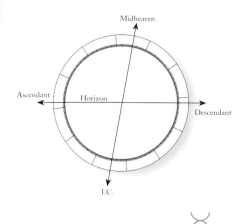

The Fixed Ascendant

Serious and deliberate, you prefer a stable lifestyle. You enjoy a fixed routine and dislike change. People perceive you as dependable and persevering. You have the ability to carry things through and your impact on the environment is spread over time. However, if you have a fickle Sun-sign your stability may not last. Even though the fixed Ascendant has more tenacity than most, slippery Sun-signs like to get out from under: the fixed Ascendant can be a very hard taskmaster indeed.

ASCENDANT IN TAURUS

Entrenched and deliberate, you approach things methodically. This is a truly *practical* Ascendant, concerned with material resources and productivity. A good worker, you can turn your hand to most practical tasks. You seek financial security. People may perceive you as somewhat on the slow and plodding side, but value you for your tenacity. You are the one who hangs on after everyone else gives up. This quality means that you stay in situations that you would be better off leaving. Disliking change, you hold on to what appears to be security – job, marriage, house – even when it is an illusion.

Both the Ascendant in Taurus and Leo love to entertain. Taurean dinner parties are gourmet affairs usually at home. Leo goes out to party. Restaurants are your playground.

ASCENDANT IN LEO

This is a larger-than-life ascendant that has to be out there making an impact. People cannot help noticing you as you majestically survey the world. A born actor, you like to entertain or instruct. You are happiest holding court. Generous and warm-hearted, you love to share your good fortune with others.

The confident face you present to the world may hide a shy interior. But you appear to be self-assured, radiating warmth out to a waiting world. Your impact on the environment is artistic and creative, although you leave sudden change to more flexible Ascendants.

The Aquarius Ascendant likes to be different. While not always as "in your face" as this, there is no doubting the impact.

ASCENDANT IN SCORPIO

With your Ascendant in Scorpio, you give nothing away. Inscrutable and secretive, you want to master your environment but reveal nothing in the process. Stubborn and determined, you achieve whatever you set out to do. This is a powerful Ascendant and you may find yourself involved in power struggles and manipulative situations. However, with devious cunning or forcefulness you will always overcome the obstacle in your path. You can see more deeply into things than most Ascendants – your insights can be put to good use in many situations.

Other people just cannot help noticing you. You radiate an attraction and a sexuality that is positively magnetic. This is a charismatic Ascendant that can push things through by sheer personality – usually forceful and some-times charming depending on the Sun-sign.

ASCENDANT IN AQUARIUS

You stand out from the crowd. You are *different*. Whether it is your clothing, hairstyle, or eccentric demeanor, you get noticed. You crackle with static electricity. You do not fit into conventional society and can be determined about getting your own way. Your stubbornness may, however, set you in a very unconventional rut, but people come round to your way of seeing things – afterward!

You have a far-sighted impact on the environment and on the community around you. You have the ability to see the changes that are needed way ahead of the rest of society, but this brings you into conflict with the status quo. The fixed nature of your Ascendant is reflected back by the resistance of other people to being compelled to see things from your perspective.

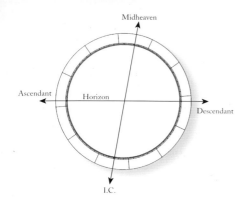

The Mutable Ascendant

With your Ascendant in a mutable sign, you are flexible and resilient. You adapt to the environment with versatility, and change does not faze you. You prefer your life to be unpredictable and rarely stick with a set routine. A mutable Ascendant can impart flexibility to the more unyielding Sun-signs.

ASCENDANT IN GEMINI

You are the communicator *par excellence*. Other people tend to notice your voice and your busy hands, or the incessant ringing of your mobile phone, before they see your face. With an insatiable curiosity, you want to report on your world. This Ascendant enjoys a good gossip. Your impact on your environment involves words, words, and more words. You always seem to know someone who can fix things.

This can be a superficial Ascendant, not liking to go too deeply into things. One manifestation of this type of ascendant is the absent-minded professor.

ASCENDANT IN VIRGO

Methodical, analytical, and dependable, you have the adaptability to respond to change, but the organization to remain in control. You are the person who is cool in a crisis and who comes up with solutions to mess and muddle; the one who can produce the facts and figures quickly – and interpret them.

This is the Ascendant characterized by service to others. You want to help humanity in whatever way you possibly can, but often this can mean getting stuck in servitude or servility rather than the true service of your ideals.

ASCENDANT IN SAGITTARIUS

What people will notice about you is the number of questions you ask. Seeking meaning, you have an overwhelming urge to explore your world. Disorganized, and characterized by scattered energy, your impact may be haphazard. Nonetheless, you manage to come up with some great ideas.

Restless and curious, this Ascendant denotes an indefatigable traveler, whether it is mental or physical. You are usually arriving, or leaving, and often keep a bag packed "just in case'.' In the bag will be the latest book, the newest theory, the most innovative philosophy, and a few old favorites as well!

ASCENDANT IN PISCES

The Ascendant in Pisces is difficult to grasp. Like an escaped bar of soap in the bath, you are hard to pin down. Fluid and ultra-adaptable, you flow through life moving this way and that as the current takes you. People notice your big eyes, and the way you gaze flatteringly at them, hanging on their every word. They think they have you hooked. Then suddenly, without warning, you are gone.

Lacking boundaries, you are sympathetic and extremely sensitive to the needs and feelings of others. One of your great problems is knowing "This is me" and distinguishing "That is you." You take on other people's feelings all too easily. This can lead to you getting pulled into victim/martyr situations when all you did was offer your help.

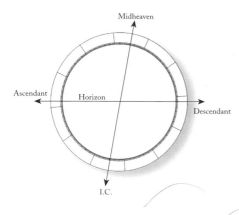

The Midheaven (MC) and the Imum Coeli (IC)

The Midheaven is what you strive for, what you reach up to. Connected to career and aspirations, it shows where you seek status and public recognition, and whether you can sustain the effort. It also indicates qualities that you value and will pursue throughout your life. The imum coeli (its opposite point) is the base of your chart. This is your roots, your family background, and your greatest security. It is introspective, introverted, and security orientated. It is where you feel safe because it is familiar and known. This is the place you withdraw to reflect on life.

THE MIDHEAVEN (MC)

Midheaven in Aries

Strives forcefully and competitively for validation, but tires easily. Values assertion and aggression. Wants personal fame. Needs challenge.

Midheaven in Taurus

Strives doggedly and determinedly for material gain. Values stability and loyalty. Wants personal security. Needs to be productive.

Midheaven in Gemini

Talks its way to the top with little staying power. Values communication and variety. Wants to be heard. Needs to satisfy curiosity.

Midheaven in Cancer

Strives with great perseverance to nurture. Values caring and concern. Wants to mother. Needs to have emotional needs met by career.

Midheaven in Leo

Proudly courts success and expects to find it with minimum effort. Values dignity. Wants to shine. Needs to find recognition.

Midheaven in Virgo

Assiduously strives to be of service. Values order and organization. Wants to be of value. Needs to contribute.

Midheaven in Libra

Languidly strives for balance. Values harmony. Wants to cooperate. Needs to be in partnership.

Midheaven in Scorpio

Resolutely strives for power. Values loyalty. Wants to get to the top. Needs intensity.

The Midheaven is where we seek status and recognition.

With the Midheaven in Aquarius, you will use protest and social revolution to put your ideals into practice.

Midheaven in Sagittarius

Fires off arrows with little thought for where they land. Values truth. Wants freedom. Needs plenty of variety.

Midheaven in Capricorn

Strives determinedly for the top. Enormous staying power. Values convention. Wants stability. Needs to be in control.

Midheaven in Aquarius

Strives for a better world. Values humanity. Wants freedom. Needs to feel accepted.

Midheaven in Pisces

Lets success slip away when nearly there. Values emotional sharing. Wants to save the world. Needs to be loved.

THE IMUM COELI (IC)

ARIES Rooted in individuality. Safe within the Self.

TAURUS Rooted in material security. Safe within stability.

GEMINI Rooted in understanding. Safe within change.

CANCER Rooted in a secure home. Safe within emotions.

LEO Rooted in the heart. Safe within specialness.

VIRGO Rooted in order. Safe within limits.

LIBRA Rooted in relationship. Safe within partnership.

SCORPIO Rooted in the depths. Safe whatever the trauma.

SAGITTARIUS Rooted in freedom. Safe when exploring.

CAPRICORN Rooted in convention. Safe within society.

AQUARIUS Rooted in liberation. Safe within equality.

PISCES Rooted in wholeness. Safe within psychic space.

At the root of the chart – the I.C. – family values are what matter.

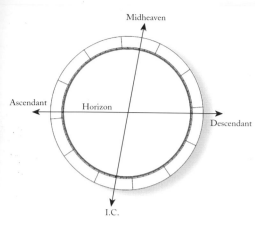

The Descendant

The Descendant (opposite your Ascendant sign on the zodiac wheel) shows how you interact with others, what you seek in a relationship, and the kind of partner who attracts you. It indicates how easily you relate to other people, whether you can see their viewpoint, and how much of yourself you give away in the process.

Aries Descendant

You find relationships difficult because your own needs are paramount and you cannot see another's point of view. You seek a strong partner who is not clingy. Partners may be egotistical.

Taurus Descendant

Relationships are important to you because they give you a sense of security. You find it difficult to adapt to someone else's needs. You seek a dependable partner. Partners may be sex-addicted.

Gemini Descendant

You enjoy superficial relationships but find it difficult to be faithful. You can listen to someone else's point of view. You seek an entertaining companion. Partners may be outrageous flirts.

Cancer Descendant

You may well find yourself mothering your partner. Emotional sharing is important to you and you want very much to meet your partner's needs. You seek a caring partner. Partners may be smothering.

Leo Descendant

You are faithful in relationships but find it difficult to adapt to your partner's point of view. You want a partner whom you can look up to and admire. Partners may be bombastic.

Virgo Descendant

You are very fussy about relationships. Partners must share your high ideals. You seek an intellectual, sensual mate. Partners may be prudish.

A romantic Descendant can bring out the Romeo in the most pragmatic Sun-sign.

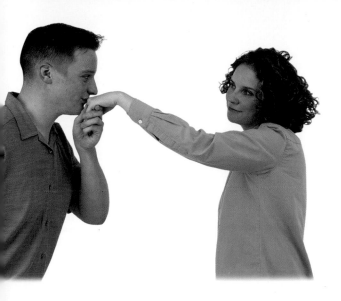

It is not just in marriage that the Descendant makes itself felt. All contracts are colored by its impulses.

Libra Descendant

Relationships are supremely important to you. You might sacrifice yourself to your partner's needs. You seek a refined partner who meets your high standards. Partners may be indecisive.

Scorpio Descendant

Relationships are intense and may be traumatic or compulsive. Empathetic, you seek a partner with whom you can explore deep emotions. Partners may have a secret.

Sagittarius Descendant

Committed relationships are difficult for you. You may not adapt easily to another's perspective. You need a partner who allows you freedom. Partners may be untrustworthy.

Relationships can end badly if the partner does not meet the Descendant's needs.

Capricorn Descendant

Your sense of responsibility makes you cautious about beginning any serious relationship. You want someone who shares your standards and conventions. Partners may be authoritarian.

Aquarius Descendant

You may enter into an unconventional type of relationship. You need to be allowed the space to be yourself within the partnership and yet may feel isolated or alone. Partners may live out your eccentricity.

Pisces Descendant

Your urge is to merge into union with your beloved. The reality is often different because you find faithfulness difficult. You seek a partner who enters your fantasy world. Partners may live out your escapist tendencies.

The Houses

In the Equal House system all the houses are the same size. The M.C. can be placed in one of several houses.

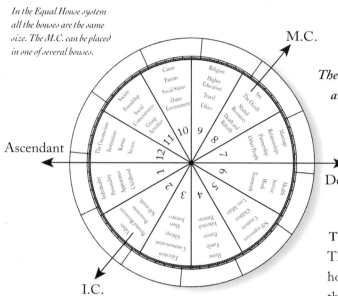

Equal house

Placidus and Koch house systems use the M.C. as the start of the tenth house. Houses are of unequal size.

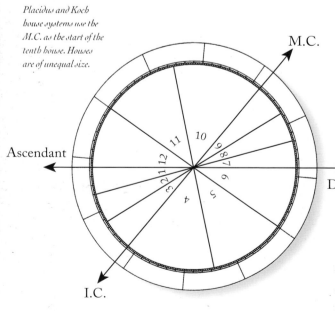

Placidus

The chart is divided into twelve houses. Houses indicate areas of life in which the planetary energies operate. They act as a focus finder and each rules a specific area. Each house encompasses at least one Zodiac sign which influences it. Not all houses will have planets within them, but some may have several planets affecting that area.

THE JOURNEY OF LIFE

The journey around a birthchart starts at the first house and moves counterclockwise. Standing on the Ascendant (the beginning of the first house) and looking out, this is what you see. It represents your individuality. Like the journey around the zodiac, the houses progress from this sense of your separate self to your contact with others, finally moving back to the whole – a journey of expanding awareness.

The houses can be looked at as a journey through time, the first house being birth and infancy, and progressing around until you reach the twelfth house, which is old age.

If you do not know your time of birth, place the Sun on the Ascendant (the start of the first house) and use that as a symbolic journey.

House systems

Astrologers use a number of methods to calculate houses. If you have a birthchart, it should tell you which house system is being used. It is more important to know which planet is in which house than to delve into the technicalities of why different methods produce slightly different results.

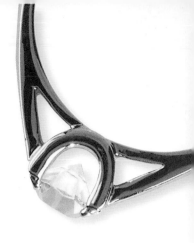

With an earth sign influencing the second house, money and valuable objects will be important to you.

THE FIRST HOUSE

The house of individuality and personality, this is the sphere of your early environment. The first house describes your experience of coming into the world, the kind of reception you had, and the conditions that surrounded you at the time. How directly you are able to express your individuality is described by the sign that begins your first house.

Any planet that is placed in the first house has a profound influence on your personality and on your early life. It will pervade your experience and expectations according to its nature.

THE SECOND HOUSE

The house of personal resources and self-worth, this is the sphere of values and possessions. The sign at the beginning of this house describes your attitude to money and the things that you own. It shows whether money comes to you easily, or is blocked. It also gives an indication of how much you value yourself.

Planets that are placed in this house describe things that come naturally to you, and indicate the type of personal resources you can draw on to make a success of life.

The first house is the first experience of life. It describes whether your birth will have been easy or fraught with difficulties, and how smoothly your early life flowed.

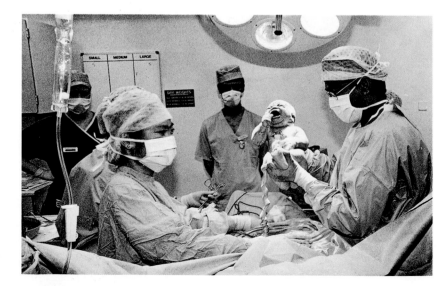

With a fire sign influencing the second house, you are likely to go for a flashy car rather than money in the bank.

THE THIRD HOUSE

The third house is the sphere of communication, where you express yourself to your immediate environment, including your siblings. Because it is where you explore your world, it includes education and short journeys.

This house describes the nature of your mind and the way that you communicate. It also shows whether you expect confusion or clear communication. The sign of the house and planets placed here can enhance or block the flow of self-expression and describe your thought processes.

THE FOURTH HOUSE

The fourth house is the sphere of the home and of the family environment. This is the base from which you move out into the world and the sign of this house indicates whether you do that confidently or fearfully. It indicates the kind of home that will make you feel secure.

This is one of the parental houses (the other being the tenth) and planets in this house describe your experience of being parented. They also describe what you expect from a parent. The parent signified by this house and the planets located here gives primary nurturing care.

With a full third house, or an air sign here, communication will be all-important – your main focus being to go out to the world.

THE FIFTH HOUSE

This is where you begin the process of moving out into the world. It is the house of creativity, leisure, and recreation. Planets in this house indicate how easily your creative urges will flow.

These urges are procreative also because this is the playful house of love affairs (not marriage) and children. Planets here show how much you are in touch with your inner child and how you express this.

THE SIXTH HOUSE

This is the house of service, health, and work. It is where you give of yourself. It is where you ask: "How can I put my talents to work?" This is work that you enjoy and do well, rather than the career you strive for. Signs and planets here show how much of yourself you sacrifice for the greater good, how unselfishly you act, and how much you are willing to share of yourself in service or in teamwork.

This is also the house of health. Planets here will describe the kind of illnesses from which you suffer and may suggest an unorthodox healing therapy to help.

With an active, outgoing sign or planet influencing the fifth house, sport or dance will be an important recreational activity. An indolent sign here will signify a couch potato.

THE SEVENTH HOUSE

The start of the seventh house is the Descendant. This is the house of relationships in the widest sense of the word. It is where you interact with, and reach out to, others. As with the Descendant, it describes what you seek from a partner and the kind of person to whom you will be attracted.

This house also describes what is reflected back to you through the eyes of another individual.

THE EIGHTH HOUSE

This is a complex house. It is the house of immortality, where you encounter sex, death, and rebirth, and where you face endings but can find regeneration. It is also where you open to another and share yourself in sexual union. And then again, it is where you share your monetary and other resources with others, and what you inherit from them.

This house represents the metaphysical realm, mysterious forces taking you on a path to higher consciousness. This is a route that may go via the mystical depths of this occult house.

Money is a feature of the eighth house. Not the earning of it, but rather the sharing or receiving.

THE NINTH HOUSE

In the philosophical ninth house you explore systems of belief and ethics. You turn to higher education to learn of other cultures. You journey to explore them for yourself – this is the house of long journeys.

Planets placed here show whether you conform to or conflict with society's mores and morality and how forcefully you are willing to impress your views onto others.

THE TENTH HOUSE

The tenth house is where you make your mark on the world. The house of career and aspirations, this sign shows how ambitious, or otherwise, you are. It also indicates what you want to be valued for, and the achievements and qualities that you feel are the important ones. Vocations and natural abilities are shown by planets found here.

This is one of the parental houses, describing the parent who had the most influence in socializing you and pushing you out into the world. The work that you do may well reflect the influence of this parent.

With an adventurous sign influencing the ninth house, you may backpack around the world. With a hedonistic sign here, it will be luxury all the way. In either case, you will grow from the journey.

THE ELEVENTH HOUSE

The eleventh house is a social house where you extend your sense of identity to become part of a greater group – whether it is cultural, racial, or global. This is the house of group interaction, the society in which you live, and the social consciousness you develop. Planets located here show how well, or otherwise, you fit into society and the type of social interaction you seek.

This is also the house of hopes and wishes, what you envision for yourself and for others. Planets in this house indicate how well those hopes can be manifested and how strongly your vision will impact on society.

THE TWELFTH HOUSE

In the hidden twelfth house dwell secrets and sacrifices. This is the house of the past and of the collective unconscious. Planets that lurk here show you your karma, the results of your past actions, and the learning process that you are undergoing. The twelfth house is also the house of institutions.

This is the house of reintegration and reconnection to the whole. When a powerful sense of individuality such as Aries has been constructed, such a merging back may be painful. Where separation has been difficult, as with Pisces, the reintegration is welcomed.

With a full tenth or eleventh house, you will want to go out to influence a waiting world.

The Aspects

Aspects are the geometric relationships that planets make to each other as they move around the zodiac. They describe how the planets interact – in harmony or in conflict. They can indicate points of psychological stress or abilities to be developed. Aspects relate to the degree of the signs in which two planets are placed. If degrees are close (within about 8°), then they are "in aspect."

Accord or discord?

The angular distance existing between the planets is known as an angle. Where planets are in a different sign but at the same degree, they are "exact aspects." However, aspects have an allowance of about 8° – an "orb" – where the influence on each other is still strong. Planets that occupy the same place in a sign are also described as being in aspect.

Aspects are divided into harmonious and tense. Planets opposite or square to each other have an innate tension, but this is not necessarily bad because conflicting energies set each other off. However, they can block the natural flow, creating difficulties in expression. Planets that fall into easier triangular relationships will be seen to flow more easily.

THE MAJOR ASPECTS

Aspects are known as major or minor. We will look at major aspects here because these have the strongest effect on how planetary energies flow.

Conjunction 0° ☌

The aspect of ease, this unites planetary energies in an immediate and visible way – unless they are embodying very different drives. If this is the case they will fight for the space to express themselves.

Sextile 60° ⚹

An aspect of ease or harmony, this creates little stress. It has less impact than other major aspects. The energies of these planets are familiar and comfortable with each other, but this aspect may prove to be a source of conflict if powerful planets are involved.

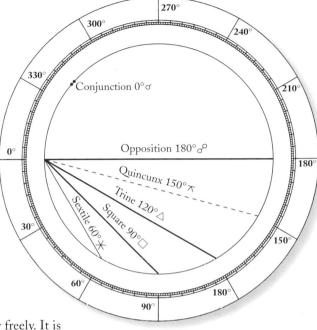

Square 90° □

An aspect of potential stress, planets in
square aspect are at odds with each other.
However, this challenge may be necessary to
get things moving. Squares can either have an
energizing effect, or may create a block.

Trine 120° △

A harmonious aspect, this allows energy to flow freely. It is
an aspect of planetary potential. Trines can be lazy, however, and
need a passing planet (a transit) to kickstart them into action.

Quincunx 150° ⚹

Although technically a minor aspect, this is in fact a point of major tension
because the energies need integration. Karmically speaking, these planetary
forces have been in conflict for a long time and need to be balanced.

Opposition 180° ☍

This is a dynamic aspect. When discordant energies are engaged in head-on
conflict, the tension that results forces a resolution. When harmonious
energies are brought face-to-face, it enlivens and strengthens them.

*Planets in harmonious
aspect with each other are
like one big happy family.*

Putting it All Together

By now you will probably be feeling that you have the pieces of a jigsaw puzzle but cannot see the whole picture. You understand the separate parts of your chart, but it is still not you yet. You do not know how to make it fit together. The art and skill of astrology lies in weighing and integrating the different factors.

DOMINANT INFLUENCES

It helps to know what the strongest energies in the horoscope are. The Sun, the fire element, positive signs, cardinal or fixed qualities, the Ascendant, and planets in the first house tend to be dominant – especially at first glance. But unconscious factors also control behavior, and the Moon and the IC may well be powerful influences under the surface. A lot depends on which signs and elements are emphasized in your chart, and which planet is making itself felt.

Pluto, Uranus, and Saturn all have a particularly powerful effect when they are placed in the first or twelfth house of the chart, but they may make themselves known in any house.

A fire Ascendant overrules a watery or airy Sun. Mars in the first house gives added drive to laid-back air or water Sun-signs. An earthy Ascendant adds a practical face to an otherwise impractical watery or fiery Sun. You can use what you have learned in this book about the elements, polarities, and qualities to measure the influence of the various signs and houses.

PLANETS IN HOUSES

You have already learned how the planets behave in signs. The houses have an affinity with signs: Aries with the first house, Taurus with the second house, Gemini with the third house, and so on. The planets are the energies that help a house to express itself. The house provides a theater of life for the planet to perform in. It helps to remember the way that planets act.

• Dominantly in the first house
• Concretely in the second house
• Mentally in the third house

You are a unique expression of a very special and particular set of energies: your birthchart. The strength of the different factors is what makes you "you."

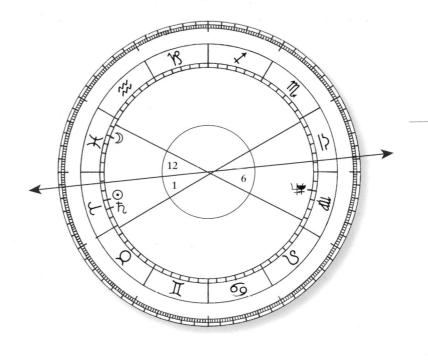

- Protectively in the fourth house
- Creatively in the fifth house
- Altruistically in the sixth house
- In partnership in the seventh house
- Intensely in the eighth house
- Philosophically in the ninth house
- Impactfully in the tenth house
- Socially in the eleventh house
- Deviously in the twelfth house

Example

With the Sun in fiery Aries in the first house and the Moon in watery Pisces in the twelfth house, the egotistical energies of the Sun predominate. But the sacrificial urge of Pisces underlies life and may be your undoing. If you add Saturn in the first house to the mix, that self-centered Aries Sun is contained, or held back. If you slip the earthed inspiration of Neptune in Virgo in the sixth house into the equation, then you may well dedicate your life to altruistic service to the underprivileged.

Charity work, overseas volunteer, or aidworker would be a typical manifestation of the energies of the example chart above.

Compatibility

Elemental attraction – red lines indicate strong attraction, purple lines weaker attraction.

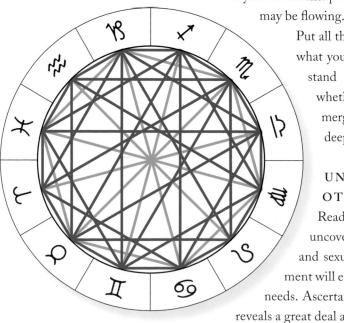

Element conflict – dark blue lines show strong conflict, pale blue lines less strong conflict.

Astrology tells you a great deal about your own emotional needs and those of other people. If you understand what you are looking for in a partner, you are more likely to be able to fulfill your needs. If you understand someone else's sexual style, then you will be able to make allowances for a different way of relating.

UNDERSTANDING YOURSELF

We all have conflicting emotional needs. You have already explored your individual emotional patterns and expectations through the Moon, Venus, and Mars, and will have identified your own personal dilemmas. In the pages that follow you will see how the Sun-signs behave in sexual relationships – whether they are faithful and loyal, or flirtatious and fickle. Reading your Sun-sign gives you a greater understanding of your relationship style, and how freely your sexual energies may be flowing.

Put all these factors together, and you can identify what you are looking for in a partner and understand your deeper emotional motivation – whether you seek security or stimulation, merging or individuality, space and freedom or deep intimacy.

UNDERSTANDING OTHER PEOPLE

Reading the Sun-sign for your partner will uncover more about his or her emotional needs and sexual style. Looking up their Moon placement will enlighten you further as to their emotional needs. Ascertaining where Venus and Mars are located reveals a great deal and brings about deeper understanding.

WHO AM I COMPATIBLE WITH?

As a general rule, you are compatible with people who have their Suns in your element. You will find emotional sympathy with those with whom you share a Moon sign or element – but conflicting Sun elements can override this, and create the "can't live with" and can't live without" syndrome.

    You are attracted to people who have the Sun, Moon, Venus, or Mars in your Sun or Descendant sign. If your Venus strongly connects with someone else's Mars, there is a powerful sexual frisson. You may be strongly attracted to someone whose Sun falls in the opposite sign on the zodiac wheel, but this attraction will contain an element of conflict, which can be exciting.

WHO SHOULD I AVOID?

Obviously, choosing someone who has totally different emotional needs and a sexual style that conflicts with yours causes problems. On the whole, some-one with the Sun in a very different element to you will be less compatible, although sharing a quality could offset this. Fire and Air elements find Earth and Water signs difficult, because the two groups have radically different approaches to life.

Fire ♈ ♌ ♐

Fire signs share a basic impulse to hunt for a mate. These predatory signs are active and enterprising in love, needing a partner who flatters and entertains – and appreciates high sexual energy. Although loyal, not all fire signs are faithful. Less active signs can be energized by a fire sign, but could find it hard to keep pace. Knowing when to opt out and relax helps you cope with high-octane fire.

There is always an element of excitement when fire signs congregate together. Passions run high!

ARIES IN LOVE

IS Aggressive. Passionate. "Me" oriented. Impulsive. Faithful but strays.

NEEDS Stimulation. Excitement. Passion.

SEX DRIVE Strong. Immediate.

LEAVES Impetuously, slams doors.

Aries with

Aries Tempestuous relationship. High sex drive and energy level.

Taurus Irresistible force meets immovable object.

Gemini Aries may incite Gemini passion, if talking stops.

Cancer Two strong-willed signs unite or fight. Aries feels smothered.

Leo King Ram meets Queen Bee. Passion or conflict?

Virgo Restrained passion offers Aries a challenge. Can you resist?

Libra "I" meets "We." Harmonious relationship results? Aries is keen to try.

Scorpio Scorpio inscrutability presents a challenge. Strong passions.

Sagittarius Mutual passion ignites but sparks can fly since Sagittarius hates being bossed around.

Capricorn Aries awakens strong passion, taking controlled Capricorn by storm.

Aquarius Passion runs high but Aries finds Aquarius too detached.

Pisces Aries finds it hard to understand the dreamy Pisces nature.

Cooler souls may be consumed by fire – or bask in its warm glow.

LEO IN LOVE

IS Warmhearted. Predatory. Exuberant. Dramatic. Proud. Bombastic. Faithful. Loyal.

NEEDS Adulation. Imagination. Prolonged foreplay.

SEX DRIVE High.

LEAVES With dignity under extreme provocation.

Leo with

Aries Aries supplies the sexual impetus Leo lacks.

Taurus Takes a long time to get going, but mutual sex drive strong.

Gemini Gemini plays courtier to Leo's king.

Cancer Leo plays head of household but may find Cancer too emotional.

Leo Is there room for two grandiose egos in one relationship?

Virgo Leo likes a willing slave. Passionate submission by Virgo helps.

Libra Both signs make high demands on partners. Can Libra keep the peace?

Scorpio Leo is attracted by that air of mystery but may find Scorpio's introversion difficult.

Sagittarius Sexual conflagration but can it last?

Capricorn Stable, loving partnership as long as Capricorn does not plunge into gloom.

Aquarius Attraction of opposites, but Leo may find Aquarius too detached.

Pisces Mutual passion but Leo is baffled by Pisces' extremes of emotion.

SAGITTARIUS IN LOVE

IS Spontaneous. Excitable. Uncommitted. Impulsive without thought. Fickle but loyal.

NEEDS Freedom. Space. Excitement. Honesty.

SEX DRIVE Strong but erratic.

LEAVES Quickly and unexpectedly.

Sagittarius with

Aries Hot and strong. Has a tendency to burn out.

Taurus Sagittarius is in too much of a hurry and can rarely wait for Taurus.

Gemini A talkative twosome. Opposites attract. Commitment is difficult.

Cancer Sagittarius can't stand being tied down and finds Cancer smothering.

Leo Powerful passions but Sagittarius finds it tedious playing faithful retainer.

Virgo Initial attraction but Sagittarius hates being criticized.

Libra Sagittarius enjoys pleasant companionship but finds commitment difficult.

Scorpio Very different styles of relating. Sagittarius hates being tied down.

Sagittarius Ideal traveling companions through life.

Capricorn Sagittarius loathes the control Capricorn tries to exert.

Aquarius A happy match. Each gives the other space.

Pisces Sagittarius finds the emotional demands hard to handle.

Earth   ♉ ♉ ♍ ♑

Strongly motivated by a need for a physical outlet for your sexual energies, you enjoy long-term, stable relationships. Your search for a suitable mate is conducted with propriety and tenacity – earth signs rarely take no for an answer. You need a partner who shares your values and longterm commitment.

TAURUS IN LOVE

IS Stable. Practical. Sensual. Stubbornly committed. Cautious. Conventional. Loyal and faithful to the end.

NEEDS Security. Comfort.

SEX DRIVE Strong with staying power.

LEAVES Very, very reluctantly.

Taurus with

Aries Taurus finds Aries headstrong and impetuous, but sex is good.

Taurus Sensual attraction. May settle into sexual inertia but never part.

Gemini Not a happy match. Taurus finds Gemini much too flighty.

Cancer Taurus enjoys the comfortable home that Cancer creates.

Leo Two fixed signs take time to get going, but partnership could last for ever.

Virgo Mutually compatible aims. Good sex life. Shared commitment

Libra Stable partnership although Taurus resists Libra's manipulative demands.

Scorpio Powerful attraction and meeting of strong sex drives.

Sagittarius Taurus finds Sagittarius too flighty but can enjoy momentary passion.

Capricorn Mutually supportive partnership. Good sex life.

Aquarius If Taurus can persuade Aquarius to commit, good match.

Pisces Pisces mystifies Taurus, who cannot handle emotional fluidity.

Sexual libido runs deep in outwardly cool earth signs but is seldom the sole motivating factor in relationships – security needs are equally important.

VIRGO IN LOVE

IS Restrained. Sensual. Prudish (or promiscuous). Idealistic. Considerate. Critical. Faithful – usually.

NEEDS Security. Perfection. Intellectual rapport.

SEX DRIVE Strong but controlled.

LEAVES After due consideration.

Virgo with

Aries Virgo attracted to Aries' energy, but dislikes self-centeredness

Taurus Excellent match. Appreciate each other's qualities.

Gemini Flexible partnership with intellectual companionship.

Cancer Virgo appreciates Cancer's homemaking, but not the emotional possessiveness.

Leo While Virgo likes to serve, constant demands for attention are wearing.

Virgo Ideal intellectual and sexual companions, but beware of mutual criticism.

Libra Virgo is a willing slave, but Libra's indecisiveness drives Virgo crazy.

Scorpio Virgo enjoys the challenge of peering under inscrutable exterior.

Sagittarius Intellectual curiosity well-matched. Virgo irritated by lack of attention to detail.

Capricorn Mutual support and understanding, and plenty of sex.

Aquarius Shared humanitarian ideals. Aquarian experimentation shocks or delights.

Pisces Mutual attraction. Pisces' lack of precision drives Virgo mad.

CAPRICORN IN LOVE

IS Controlled. Status-conscious. Restrained. Persevering. Faithful but not above trophy affairs.

NEEDS Stability. Routine.

SEX DRIVE Strong when feeling safe.

LEAVES Reluctantly.

Capricorn with

Aries Share ambition and strong sex drive. Capricorn wants to control.

Taurus Capricorn appreciates dependable support on the way to the top.

Gemini Capricorn finds Gemini much too fickle. Shallow chatter irritates Capricorn.

Cancer Cancer is happy to support Capricorn, providing stable homelife.

Leo Leo's warm heart may thaw Capricorn's apparent coldness.

Virgo Virgo prepared to become a slave to Capricorn's ambition.

Libra Mutual desire for stability, but Libra's indecisiveness a problem.

Scorpio Capricorn finds sexual intensity intriguing, but is challenged by deep emotions.

Sagittarius Serious Capricorn finds Sagittarius too casual.

Capricorn Marriage made in heaven, mutually supportive and sexual.

Aquarius Capricorn finds Aquarius' unconventionality difficult.

Pisces Capricorn does not know how to deal with Pisces' fluidity or emotionality.

121

Air ♊ ♎ ♒

Yours is a fickle, flirtatious nature, enjoying the social aspect of dating. Constant stimulation avoids boredom, so you may change partners frequently. Your sexual energy is erratic and mentally based. Friendship is as important to you as sexual attraction in making the decision to commit. You need a companion who shares your wide-ranging interests – or is happy to remain at home, alone.

GEMINI IN LOVE

IS Charming. Changeable. Uncommitted. Flirtatious. Fickle.

NEEDS Communication. Mental stimulation. Companionship.

SEX DRIVE Erratic, easily sidetracked.

LEAVES Speedily and surreptitiously.

Romance, flirtation, and conversation. Air signs take a lighthearted approach to relationships and thoroughly enjoy the trappings of courtship.

Gemini with

Aries Initial attraction, but Gemini finds Aries too bossy.

Taurus Gemini finds Taurus boring.

Gemini All talk and little sexual action.

Cancer Gemini cannot handle Cancer's possessiveness.

Leo Gemini finds Leo's need for attention too demanding.

Virgo Good intellectual companions. Might talk Gemini into bed.

Libra Gemini finds Libra's thought processes fascinating.

Scorpio Scorpio's depth fascinates Gemini, but finds the emotional intensity frightening.

Sagittarius Mutual attraction as Sagittarius sweeps Gemini into bed.

Capricorn Gemini finds Capricorn far too serious.

Aquarius Aquarius' ideals interest Gemini. Mental sparks fly.

Pisces Gemini is seduced by Pisces' mysticism, but fears engulfment.

Air signs often have their heads too much in the clouds to feel the gut-level of hot physical sexual attraction – until forcefully reminded.

LIBRA IN LOVE

IS Equable. Poised. Charming. Laid-back. In love with love. Seductive. Flirtatious. Considerate. Surprisingly fickle.

NEEDS Harmony. Partnership. Romantic love.

SEX DRIVE Gentle.

LEAVES Diplomatically.

Libra with

Aries Fatal attraction. Aries may be too coarse for refined Libra.

Gemini Libra easily succumbs to Gemini's honeyed words.

Taurus Libra appreciates Taurus' staying power.

Cancer A great deal of energy goes into the home, some of it may be apparent in the bedroom.

Leo Mutual admiration society, or attention-seeking ploys.

Virgo Peace-loving Libra finds Virgo too fussy and pedantic.

Libra Two halves of a whole. The perfect relationship?

Scorpio May be too intense for laid-back Libra to handle.

Sagittarius Mutual attraction, but will they settle down together?

Capricorn Ambition combines with stable partnership.

Aquarius Mental empathy can bring harmony.

Pisces These two enjoy mutual fantasies of eternal domestic bliss.

AQUARIUS IN LOVE

IS Unconventional. Detached: acts as though observing alien species. Once committed, remains that way.

NEEDS Freedom. Space. An understanding partner.

SEX DRIVE Light.

LEAVES When deeply committed, reluctantly.

Aquarius with

Aries Humanitarian and individualistic. Can they combine ideals?

Gemini Mutual fascination with ideals. Is Gemini too fickle?

Taurus Two fixed signs may give it a try, if Taurus can avoid possessiveness.

Cancer Cancer's emotional possessiveness is off-putting for Aquarius.

Leo Opposites attract. Can they find mutual understanding?

Virgo Mutual ideals of service bring these two together.

Libra May complement each other if Aquarius can commit.

Scorpio Can be a powerful combination.

Sagittarius Free spirits understand each other. Give each other sufficient space.

Capricorn Aquarius finds Capricorn too stuffy.

Aquarius It takes one Aquarian to understand another. But can they find mutual commitment?

Pisces Aquarius finds Pisces' escapism difficult.

Water ♋ ♏ ♓

The fluid water element flows where emotional currents dictate, seeking a mate who feels right. You value partnership and dream of romantic love. Your unconscious needs can trap you in inappropriate relationships. With your ideal mate you are loyal, with strong sexual energy. Most of the water signs wear rose-colored glasses when looking at love.

The water signs flow in and out of relationship with consummate ease. Love is what makes the world go round for these sentimental souls.

CANCER IN LOVE

IS Emotional. Possessive. Nurturing. Tender. Considerate. Jealous. Faithful and loyal.

NEEDS Safety. Emotional empathy. A home. The prospect of children

SEX DRIVE Strong but oblique behind a cool facade.

LEAVES Cancer stays!

Cancer with

Aries Powerful sex drive, but Cancer needs emotional sharing.

Gemini Neither understands where the other is coming from.

Taurus May settle down together. Demand mutual faithfulness.

Cancer Too busy emoting to do much relating. Mutual dependence holds tightly.

Leo Cancer is pleased to nurture but emotional gap emerges.

Virgo Mutual criticism mars an otherwise good relationship.

Libra Mutual values, but Libra may be too fickle for possessive Cancer.

Scorpio Deep emotions flow under an apparently serene surface.

Sagittarius Cancer cannot cope with Sagittarius' need for space.

Capricorn Excellent partnership. Mutual support society.

Aquarius This can be a surprisingly happy pairing.

Pisces Emotionally sympathetic, but Cancer finds Pisces' escape bids threatening.

All the water signs find being on or near water relaxing and refreshing. This is the perfect spot for a romantic tryst.

SCORPIO IN LOVE

IS Sexy. Intense. Secretive. Charismatic. Plays power games. Jealous. Faithful – usually!

NEEDS Security. Passion. Emotional bonding. Loyalty.

SEX DRIVE Powerful below surface.

LEAVES Traumatically after brooding deeply.

Scorpio with

Aries Challenging but highly passionate. Scorpio hates to be pressured.

Taurus Magnetic attraction. Solid union.

Gemini Scorpio finds Gemini too slippery to pin down.

Cancer Deep emotional waters, very possessive but empathetic.

Leo Powerful stuff. This relationship could last – or explode.

Virgo Sensual, but Scorpio pushes Virgo to the emotional limits.

Libra Powerful union if Libra acquiesces. Lifelong partnership could result.

Scorpio Highly charged and intense. May sting each other to death!

Sagittarius Scorpio finds Sagittarius hot stuff but too fickle.

Capricorn Strong stuff but control issues abound. It may be worth it for the passion!

Aquarius Electric attraction. Aquarius will have to be faithful.

Pisces Deep emotional waters, but can Scorpio cope with Pisces' mutability?

PISCES IN LOVE

IS Vacillating. Idealistic. Emotional. Gullible. Seductive. Promiscuous. Rescuer. Fickle.

NEEDS Union. Merging. To feel needed. Emotional bonds. Fantasy.

SEX DRIVE Flows where it will.

LEAVES Rarely. You remain emotionally entangled with past lovers.

Pisces with

Aries May engage in a delightful fantasy.

Taurus Water flowing around a solid rock. Could work.

Gemini Understand each other's restlessness, but Pisces needs emotional bonding.

Cancer Precisely the kind of emotional symbiosis both crave.

Leo Pisces may adore, but swims off in search of other fish sooner or later.

Virgo Mutual attraction. Complementary qualities cement relationship.

Libra Both sides want to lose themselves in another person.

Scorpio Magnetic attraction, but can Pisces cope with the jealousy?

Sagittarius May start with steam but water soon douses the fire.

Capricorn Earth energy may ground Pisces, but Pisces hates control.

Aquarius May enjoy sexual experimentation and bizarre fantasy.

Pisces Total emotional submersion. Will they ever be separate again?

Looking to the Future

When you read your newspaper horoscope, it will often refer to the day-to-day movements of the planets (called transits). Phrases such as "With Mars moving through your sign," "Pluto has just entered your sign," or, "Saturn is in the opposite sign," are used to explain why certain events are taking place.

PINPOINTING CHANGE

Traditionally, astrology was used to predict the future. Today, transits are used to pinpoint periods of change such as a major career move, a new house, a fresh relationship, or the unfolding of inner growth.

Transits are times of change and activation. Although the planets do not actually cause anything to happen, *it feels as though they do*. When they move through your sign or make a strong relationship with a planet in your birthchart, the energies of that sign or planet are activated. If Mars happens to be visiting your sign, you suddenly get more energetic or may feel as though you have been given a kickstart.

Timing

Day-to-day movements of the planets affect your life for a very short time if they are personal planets, or for up to two years in the case of heavyweight outer planets. When these latter planets are on the move, you can feel the effect for up to six months before it actually occurs. The actual transit lasts six months to a year, and then it takes at least another six months to integrate the effects. Consulting an astrologer is one way to foresee these events, but if you do read your horoscope regularly, you will be given due warning of impending visits.

Age-related transits

Certain planets have an effect at a particular stage in life or at a certain age (*See* Saturn, Jupiter, Uranus, and Chiron). The Saturn Return (at age 28-9 and 57) is a period of major reassessment. The Uranus Opposition (mid-40s) is a time of drastic change or stress.

Most people like to glance at their "stars" but for a proper forecast an astrologer is a much better guide to what the planets have in store for you.

THE MOON EFFECT

There is an astrological planet that effects you for a short time every month. For two and a half days, the Moon moves through your Sun-sign, bringing any underlying emotional issues to the surface (*See* the Moon Tables on pages 60–3. These tell you when this will take place).

Twice a year, a new Moon or a full Moon in your Sun- and Moon-signs will affect you strongly. (Glancing at the sky tells you the phase of the Moon, the Moon Tables tells you the sign). The new Moon completes one cycle and starts off another – time to let go of the past and make a new beginning.

At the full Moon projects come to fruition. However, "Full Moon Madness" is not just an old wives' tale. The full Moon may well bring about a crisis in your emotional life and you may appear to be behaving irrationally: you are not – it is just that you can no longer repress those feelings any longer! Recognizing and accepting what is happening goes a long way toward dealing with it.

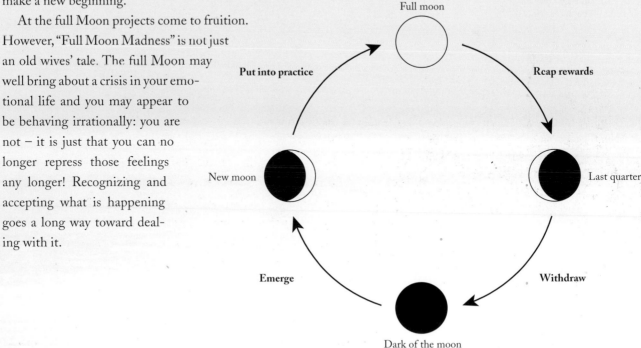

Full moon

Put into practice

Reap rewards

New moon

Last quarter

Emerge

Withdraw

Dark of the moon

Process and dream

Index

HOW TO OBTAIN A BIRTHCHART
COMPUTER CHARTS
78 Neal Street, Covent Garden,
London WC2H 9PA, England
Tel: 011 44 171 497 1001
Fax: 011 44 171 497 0344
Astrolabe PO Box 1750 350 Underpass
Road Brewster, MA 02631.
Tel: (508) 896-5081
Fax: (508) 896-5289.
ASTROCARTOGRAPHY CHARTS
Equinox 78 Neal Street, Covent
Garden London WC2H 9PA
Tel: 011 44 171 497 1001
Fax: 011 44 171 497 0344
Astro Numeric Service
Box 336-r Ashland, OR 97520
1-800 Mapping

The publishers are grateful to the following for permission to reproduce
copyright material:

AKG: 9TL, 9R, 28, 30L, 32L, 36L,
59, 70/71, 82B; **Bridgeman Art
Library:** 74, 75R, 87BR, 90/91;
Britstock-IFA: 69BR, 92C, 100L; **e.t.
Archive:** 7TR, 26L, 40L, 66L, 69T,
71R, 73R, 81T, 87TL; **Hulton:** 33BR,
38BL, 111BL; **Images:** 2; **Kobal
Collection:** 33T, 33TR, 74/75, 125T;
Panos: 115BR; **Rex Features:** 33BR,
77R, 85BR, 101T; **Science Photo
Library:** 20l, 22, 25T, 70L, 72L,
76/77, 82TL, 84TR, 84/85, 86TL;
Stock Market: 71TR, 92; **Tony
Stone:** 6, 7BR, 9, 15, 19TL, 20BR,
25BR, 27T, 27B, 29T, 29B, 35B, 37T,
40/41, 41T, 42L, 44L, 47BR, 51TR,
51BR, 60TL, 64TL, 74, 76L, 78L,
79TR, 81B, 83T, 84L, 87BR, 92TL,
95TL, 96BL, 97, 99TR, 99B, 101BR,
102L, 106L, 107TR, 107BR, 108,
109BR, 110T, 110/111, 111BR, 112,
118L, 119, 121T, 123, 124L, 127;
Trip: 51TR